THE
DREAMKEEPERS

THE DREAMKEEPERS

SUCCESSFUL TEACHERS OF AFRICAN AMERICAN CHILDREN

SECOND EDITION

Gloria Ladson-Billings

JB JOSSEY-BASS™
A Wiley Brand

Published by Jossey-Bass
A Wiley Imprint
989 Market Street, San Francisco, CA 94103-1741—www.josseybass.com

Tables 3.1, 4.1, and 5.1 are reprinted from Ladson-Billings, G. "Like Lightning in a Bottle: Attempting to Capture the Pedagogical Excellence of Successful Teachers of Black Students." QSE, 3(4), 335–344. Reprinted with permission.

The epigraph on p. 127 is from On the Pulse of Morning. Reprinted with permission of Random House, Inc.

Cover design by Paula Schlosser.
Front cover photograph © Nita Winter, Corte Madera, California.

Jossey-Bass books and products are available through most bookstores. To contact Jossey-Bass directly call our Customer Care Department within the U.S. at 800-956-7739, outside the U.S. at 317-572-3986, or fax 317-572-4002.

Jossey-Bass also publishes its books in a variety of electronic formats. Some content that appears in print may not be available in electronic books.

Library of Congress Cataloging-in-Publication Data
Ladson-Billings, Gloria, 1947-
   The dreamkeepers : successful teachers of African American children / Gloria Ladson-Billings.
       p.   cm.
   Includes bibliographical references and index.
   ISBN 978-0-470-40815-5 (pbk.)
       1. African Americans—Education.   2. Teaching.   3. Educational anthropology—United States.   I. Title.
   LC2717.L33   2009
   371.829'96073—dc22

                                                                           2008055675

Printed in the United States of America
SECOND EDITION
PB Printing   SKY10020807_082720

CONTENTS

Foreword to the New Edition		vii
Preface		xv
The Author		xxi
1	A Dream Deferred	1
2	Does Culture Matter?	17
3	Seeing Color, Seeing Culture	33
4	We Are Family	59
5	The Tree of Knowledge	85
6	Culturally Relevant Teaching	111
7	Making Dreams into Reality	139
	Afterword	157
	Appendix A: Methodology	179
	Appendix B: Context	193
	Notes	203
	Index	217
	Discussion Questions	221

FOREWORD TO THE NEW EDITION

It may be those who do most dream most.

—STEPHEN LEACOCK

It is hard to believe that seventeen years have passed since I left the classrooms of eight wonderful teachers I called the "Dreamkeepers." Their stories have been read by thousands of pre-service, in-service, and community teachers, as well as graduate students and would-be teacher educators. The names of Gertrude Winston, Ann Lewis, Elizabeth Harris, Julia Devereaux, Patricia Hilliard, Peggy Valentine, Margaret Rossi, and Pauline Dupree have spread across the country and around the world.[1]

What Happens When We Get It Right?

In the original study I set out to demonstrate that there were teachers who were capable of teaching African American students to high levels of proficiency. Most of the scholarly literature positions African American students as problems and seeks to determine what is wrong—with their education, their families, their culture, and their minds. I wanted to ask another question, a question that would explore success models. I wanted to know what was *right* with African American students' education and what happens in classrooms where teachers, students, and parents seem to get it right. I searched for these teachers by polling African American parents, and their straightforward answers helped me find an extraordinary group of teachers. As a crosscheck I asked principals and colleagues at schools in the district to recommend outstanding teachers to me. If a teacher's name appeared on both lists—that from the parents and that from the administrators and colleagues—she became a candidate for the study.

The most memorable thing about these teachers was that they had such few obvious similarities. True, they were all women, but I presume that to be an artifact of elementary teaching (many more women teach in elementary schools than men). But there were few other characteristics that held them together. Five of the women were African American and three were white. They attended a variety of colleges and universities and came from a variety of geographic regions. After three years of working with these teachers I found two qualities that may explain their success. The first was experience. These women were very experienced teachers. None had fewer than twelve years of teaching experience. Of course we know of many teachers who have been teaching a very long time and still struggle to be effective with African American students. In a subsequent study I demonstrated that it was possible for relatively inexperienced teachers to be effective in classrooms with diverse groups of students.[2]

The second and perhaps more compelling factor was that each of these teachers could point to a transformative moment in their lives that forced them to reassess the way they did their work. Several of the teachers referenced their work in the civil rights movement. Another spoke of her experience in the Peace Corps. Still another talked of a crisis of faith that forced her to leave her religious order. These moments of transformation stand in stark contrast to the experiences of well-intentioned young people who come into teaching every year hoping to do some good for those "poor Black children." In my subsequent study with novice teachers I realized that it was important to select candidates who already had some life experiences that forced them to look closely at their lives and the lives of those less fortunate than they.

The Dreamkeepers Revisited

I maintain a relationship with a number of the women from the first study. Gertrude retired in the midst of the study (although she continued to participate in the research collaborative). She continues to send me a Christmas card every year complete with her handwritten Christmas letter. During a year's study leave from 2003 to 2004 I returned to the community where I conducted the original study. I called Gertrude and we talked on the phone but had trouble coordinating our busy schedules for a lunch meeting. Patricia Hilliard has retired. I ran into her at a community health fair and 5K walk. Although retired, she was continuing to volunteer to help children learn to read in her community. Julia Devereaux called me soon after learning I had returned to the area and invited me to be a judge for a "fancy hat" contest at a fund-raiser for her church. I saw Ms. Dupree at church and learned that she was completing her final year before retirement. I also learned that she was battling breast cancer, a disease I, too, had survived, so we had lots to talk about regarding treatments, therapies, and prognosis. Ann Lewis, Margaret Rossi, and Peggy Valentine had moved out of the area and were teaching in other communities.

The year before I returned to the community I received a call from the district's superintendent who knew about my work with the teachers in the Dreamkeepers' study. She contacted me to let me know that Elizabeth Harris, who had retired the year before, had died from a massive stroke. Her family knew of her participation in the study and the acclaim that had come to her because of it. The superintendent asked if I would identify a passage of the book that described her and her work. My first inclination was to decline her request because of research ethics, but in truth, the descriptions of the teachers were so vivid that their colleagues already knew who they were. The superintendent indicated that Mrs. Harris's family wanted to identify a section of the book to be read as a part of her eulogy. I felt that Mrs. Harris's death changed the ground rules, and this was one thing I could do to honor her wonderful work as a teacher.

Lessons Learned

As you will see in this book, there were some central conceptions that were shared by the teachers in this study. I learned that they held specific conceptions of themselves and others, that is, they strongly identified with the profession and felt it important to embrace the children in their classroom as learners. Rarely did the teachers express pity for their students, even in the case of one teacher who had a student in her classroom who became homeless and was living with his mother and brother in a car. Despite this tough situation, she found ways to keep his school life more normal and steady.

I also learned that the teachers had specific conceptions of the social relations that are to take place in a classroom. They worked to create a community of learners instead of idiosyncratic connections with students they favored. This community building was almost always a result of deliberate pedagogical strategies the teachers used. For one teacher it was the class camping trip. For another teacher it was describing and referring to the class members as "family members." Over and over the teachers emphasized collective responsibility and collective rewards.

Third, I learned that the teachers held conceptions of knowledge that were different from many of their colleagues. For these teachers knowledge was flexible and contestable. Just because something appeared in a textbook they did not feel obligated to accept it. They were careful to search for the warrants that supported curriculum assertions, and they regularly vetted materials by looking for other ways to substantiate claims. As a consequence they expected students to do the same. They did not want their students to just receive or consume knowledge. They wanted them to be able to produce knowledge, and their demands for success were evident in how they taught.

What to Teach Versus How to Teach

The eight teachers I studied focused on three central things in their teaching, even though their specific methodologies may have varied greatly. All eight teachers had a strong focus on student learning, developing cultural competence, and cultivating a sociopolitical awareness in their students. Student learning was varied and multifaceted in their classrooms. It was not demonstrated merely as a score on a standardized test. Instead students were encouraged to demonstrate what they knew in writing, speaking, and a variety of exhibitions.

Cultural competence was an important source of connection between the teachers and their students. They believed it was important that the students were well grounded in their own culture as a prerequisite to becoming versed in what might be considered mainstream culture. African American history, literature, art, music, dance, and perspectives were a big part of the curriculum. These perspectives were examined alongside other perspectives so that students could see the various ways different groups made sense of the world. Students in these teachers' classrooms were often asked to explore multiple perspectives as they bolstered their own knowledge and skills.

Finally, the teachers insisted that students understood the sociopolitical underpinnings of their schooling experience. Students looked at community, state, national, and global issues and raised questions about how what they were learning in school had a larger payoff. Instead of "Why do we have to learn this stuff?" students in these teachers' classrooms were regularly pushed to make a connection between their in-school lives and their out-of-school experiences.

Keeping the Dream Alive

At the end of this book, I profile a new generation of Dreamkeepers—young teachers who are carrying out their work with the same levels of dedication and excellence as the original eight Dreamkeepers. To give you a preview of these teachers, I offer a profile of one I call Myesha Jordan, and I would like to start her story from the end. Myesha is currently a teacher educator in the South. She completed her degree at one of the nation's top colleges of education. The program is highly competitive and respected among the top ten in the nation. Before returning to complete her Ph.D. in English education, Myesha was a well-respected middle school English teacher. One of the top literacy researchers in the country was conducting research in her classroom because she was an outstanding teacher. I watched Myesha's teaching on film and saw some very familiar interactions between her and her students. She was tearing out a page from The Dreamkeepers and applying her own personality and style. Instead of reducing her instruction to the lowest common denominator of teaching to the test as so many of her colleagues did, Myesha insisted on teaching students using big ideas and powerful concepts that forced them to think and not merely react. For example, Myesha often started her teaching with "big questions" such as "Why do adults dislike youth culture?" This question forced the students to look both at current-day youth trends and youth trends over time. Students explored 1920s trends such as swallowing goldfish and 1950s trends such as stuffing teens in phone booths next to current-day trends of wearing baggy pants or getting tattoos.

Myesha learned to teach in this way not just from her teacher preparation program but because twenty years ago Myesha had the privilege of being a student in two of those original eight teachers' classrooms. Myesha was a student of Julia Devereaux and Gertrude Winston. She knew exactly what it meant to persist with students even when it seemed they were not going to make it. She knew how to cajole, push, and demand on one side while encouraging, cheering, and supporting on the other. She saw Mrs. Devereaux do it and she saw Miss Winston do it. They were her models, and when she opened the pages of *The Dreamkeepers* as a graduate student she recognized them immediately. When she and I met up at an English teachers' conference she bubbled with excitement about these women who were her mentors. Even though she had moved half way across the country, she carried their lessons with her over time and space. And, now she was the embodiment of everything they had tried to do—give back to a community that desperately needed teachers who would stop at nothing to ensure the success of every student.

I have often thought about what it would take to replicate the original Dreamkeepers study. Could I be as unobtrusive as I was nineteen years ago when I first walked into those eight class-rooms? Could I go into new classrooms without comparing this new group of teachers to the ones who have become proto-types for teaching excellence? I do not think I could. Instead I have to count on readers to minimize the effects of time and see some of the timeless qualities of those eight teachers who have become real to many teachers and prospective teachers. I have to challenge teachers to look at the eight original Dreamkeepers as models they can and should emulate even in the midst of an environment of teaching to the test. Today's teacher must ask, "What is it about Mrs. Dupree or Mrs. Harris that can help me do my work?" "What is significant about Mrs. Lewis's approach to literacy or Miss Winston's outstanding rapport with parents that can improve my practice?" "How can I make their work live on?"

PREFACE

✳

No challenge has been more daunting than that of improving the academic achievement of African American students. Burdened with a history that includes the denial of education, separate and unequal education, and relegation to unsafe, sub-standard inner-city schools, the quest for quality education remains an elusive dream for the African American community. However, it does remain a dream—perhaps the most powerful for the people of African descent in this nation.

The power and persistence of the metaphor of the dream has defined the sojourn of African Americans in the United States. From the words of the Bible to the poetry of Langston Hughes to the oratory of Martin Luther King, Jr., African Americans' struggle against all odds has been spurred on by the pursuit of a dream.

Perceived as the most direct avenue to the realization of the dream, education and access to schooling have been cherished privileges among African Americans. Slaves were not allowed to learn to read or be educated, and this has underscored the possibility and power of education for liberation. The chronicle of the civil rights movement in the United States illustrates the centrality of education to the fight of African Americans for equal opportunity and full citizenship. Thus, Central High School in Little Rock, Arkansas; the University of Mississippi; the University of Alabama; the Boston Public Schools; and Brownsville, New York, all symbolize the willingness of African Americans to sacrifice all for the sake of education.

But today African Americans find themselves in a downward spiral. African American students lag far behind their white counterparts on standard academic achievement measures. At the same time, the very society that experienced a civil rights revolution finds itself locked in the grips of racism and discrimination. Almost forty years after a Supreme Court decision declaring separate but equal schools to be illegal, most African American students still attend schools that are in reality segregated and unequal.

However, *The Dreamkeepers* is not about the despair. Rather, it is about keeping the dream alive. The significance of this book can be found in the changing demographics of our nation's public schools. Children of color constitute an increasing proportion of our students. They represent 30 percent of our public school population. In the twenty largest school districts, they make up over 70 percent of total school enrollment. Conversely, the number of teachers of color, particularly African American, is dwindling. African American teachers make up less than 5 percent of the total public school teaching population. Further, many teachers—white and black alike—feel ill-prepared for or incapable of meeting the educational needs of African American students.

Based on a study of a group of excellent teachers, this book provides exemplars of effective teaching for African American students. Rather than a prescription or a recipe, this book offers the reader models for improving practice and developing grounded theory, through a look at the intellectually rigorous and challenging classrooms of these teachers in a low-income, predominantly African American school district.

I have written this book with three voices: that of an African American scholar and researcher; that of an African American teacher; and that of an African American woman, parent, and community member. Thus the book offers a mixture of scholarship and story—of qualitative research and lived reality. I have relied heavily on "story" as a means of conveying the excellent pedagogical practice of the teachers studied. Increasingly, in fields such as law, education, ethnic studies, and feminist studies, story has gained credence as an appropriate methodology for transmitting the richness and complexity of cultural and social phenomena. Thus the audience for this book may be broad and varied.

The book is both reflective and empirical. At its center is the story of the pedagogical practice of eight exemplary teachers. However, my own experiences as an African American student who successfully negotiated public schooling provide a backdrop for my understanding of that practice. What was there in my schooling experiences that allowed me to persevere and prevail? I am not dismissing the fact that my schooling took place in a different and, perhaps, simpler time. Yet I retain vivid memories of ways in which schooling affected me both positively and negatively, and those memories help me see and understand current classroom practices.

Because of my decision to write in this way I break at least two scholarly conventions. First, I diminish the primacy of "objectivity" as I write both of my own life and memories as an African American student and of the lives and experiences of this group of effective teachers. Second, I write in a style that may be seen as methodologically "messy," as I discuss issues at both the classroom level and the school level. I do this because it is an opportunity to reinforce the fluidity and connection between the individual and the group in which teachers and students do their work.

I could have chosen to write this book in the dominant scholarly tradition—statement of the problem, review of the literature, methodology, data collection, analysis, and implications for further research. Indeed, this is what I was trained to do. But that tradition rejects my necessary subjectivity. Thus I chose to integrate my "scholarly" tools with my knowledge of my culture and my personal experiences.

Multicultural teacher educators will find this book a useful addition to the literature on curricular and instructional issues concerning African American students. Practicing teachers and student teachers will have an opportunity to create appropriate strategies and techniques for their own classrooms based on those shown in this book. Parents and community members will be able to use the book as a "talking point" to help outline the redesign of community schools that better meet the needs of their students.

However, again, the book is not a prescription. It does not contain lists of things to do to achieve effective teaching for African American students. As tempting as it was for me to do just that, my work on this book has convinced me that doing so would be professionally dishonest. I am committed to the belief that just as we expect children to extrapolate larger life lessons from the stories we tell them, we, as adults, can make our own sense of these teachers' stories about themselves and their teaching.

I have written this book not to offer a solution to problems in the education of African Americans but to offer an opportunity to make those problems central to the debate about education in general. In accordance with current public policy thinking, this book contends that the way a problem is defined frames the universe of reasonable public actions. Given our limited ability to address every problem that confronts the society, problem formulation takes on added proportions. Thus a specific problem, such as education, cannot stand alone; rather, it must be linked to broader issues like national defense, economic competitiveness, or crime. In this book, I attempt to reformulate what has been thought of as the problem of African American schooling into the promise of successful practice and the problem of our inability to consider how we might learn from that success.

This book discusses the notion of culturally relevant teaching and its inherent conceptions of the teacher and others; of classroom social interactions; of literacy and mathematics teaching; and of knowledge itself. Further, the book examines the implications of culturally relevant teaching for African American student education and teacher education.

Chapter One, in an attempt to rethink teaching and learning for African Americans, asks the question, "Is there a case for separate schools?" Far from suggesting a return to racial segregation, the chapter points to the growing disaffection of African Americans with the kind of education their children receive today in the public schools. Placed in a historical context, the question raises additional questions about teacher preparation.

Chapter Two discusses the growing educational and anthropological literature on ways in which school can be made more compatible with the students' cultural backgrounds. The chapter identifies a lack in the literature on the experiences of African American students specifically, and offers culturally relevant teaching as a way to address this gap. The chapter also compares assimilationist, or traditional, teaching practices, with culturally relevant teaching practices.

Chapter Three discusses a critical aspect of culturally relevant teaching: the teachers' conceptions of themselves and others. Vignettes and interviews with this group of successful teachers of African American students illustrate how they see themselves and their students.

Chapter Four discusses a second critical aspect of culturally relevant teaching: the manner in which classroom social interactions are structured. Once again, vignettes and interview data illustrate the pertinent points.

Chapter Five discusses the third critical aspect of culturally relevant teaching: the teachers' conception of knowledge. The chapter provides examples of how this kind of teaching practice helps both teachers and students construct knowledge and move beyond the state- and district-required curricula to achieve academic and cultural excellence.

Chapter Six focuses on three of the teachers in the study and their teaching of elementary literacy and mathematics programs. The focus on literacy contrasts two different instructional approaches and materials that yield similar results: a classroom of literate students. The chapter discusses the ways in which the teachers' use of culturally relevant teaching transcends the material and instructional strategy. The focus on mathematics contrasts the practice of a culturally relevant teacher with that of a novice who works in an upper middle class white school.

Chapter Seven attempts to peek into the future. It examines the prospects for improving the academic performance and the school experiences of African American students. It looks at current practice in teacher education, established school and community programs that have a focus on African American learners, and some experimental programs.

Two appendixes at the close of the book address methodological and contextual issues. They are included to help colleagues think about ways to both replicate and improve upon my research. Indeed, this entire effort represents not a conclusion but a starting point from which the educational needs of African American students can begin to be addressed.

Acknowledgments

Mere words do little to express my gratitude for the invaluable assistance I received in conceiving, developing, and writing this book. My colleagues, Mary E. Gomez, Carl A. Grant, Joyce E. King, B. Robert Tabachnick, and William H. Tate have provided me with invaluable feedback and encouragement. The National Academy of Education postdoctoral fellowship program, administered through the Spencer Foundation, gave me the resources and the opportunity to carry out the research upon which this book is based. The spiritual guidance of the Reverend and Mrs. Emil M. Thomas kept me from feeling discouraged and defeated during a period of serious illness. The teachers, parents, students, and community in which I did my research gave generously of their time and energy to make this project happen. And my family—my husband, Charles, and my children, Jessica and Kevin—gave me the time and the support to make this book a reality.

In the final analysis, however, I assume full responsibility for the contents of this book. The ideas and opinions expressed and the mistakes made are mine alone.

Madison, Wisconsin   Gloria Ladson-Billings

THE AUTHOR

Gloria Ladson-Billings is the Kellner Family Professor of Urban Education in the Department of Curriculum and Instruction and Faculty Affiliate in the Department of Educational Policy Studies at the University of Wisconsin-Madison. She is the 2005–2006 president of the American Educational Research Association. Ladson-Billings' research examines the pedagogical practices of teachers who are successful with African American students. She also investigates Critical Race Theory applications to education.

Ladson-Billings is the author of the critically acclaimed books, *The Dreamkeepers: Successful Teachers of African American Children*, *Crossing over to Canaan: The Journey of New Teachers in Diverse Classrooms*, and *Beyond the Big House: African American Educators on Teacher Education*, and more than 50 journal articles and book chapters. She is the former editor of the *American Educational Research Journal* and a member of several editorial boards. Her work has won numerous scholarly awards, including the H. I. Romnes Faculty Fellowship, the Spencer Post-doctoral Fellowship, and the Palmer O. Johnson outstanding research award. In 2002 she was awarded an honorary doctorate from Umeå University, Umeå, Sweden. During the 2003–2004 academic year she was a fellow at the Center for Advanced Study in the Behavioral Sciences, Stanford, California. In fall 2004 she received the George and Louise Spindler Award from the Council on Anthropology and Education for significant and ongoing contributions to the field of educational anthropology. In spring 2005 she was elected to the National Academy of Education and the National Society for the Study of Education. She is a 2008 recipient of the state of Wisconsin's Martin Luther King Jr. Heritage Award and the Teachers College, Columbia University, 2008 Distinguished Service Medal. During the 2008–2009 year she was named the Helen LeBaron Hilton Distinguished Chair of the Iowa State University College of Human Sciences.

THE DREAMKEEPERS

A Dream Deferred

What happens to a dream deferred?
                    —LANGSTON HUGHES

In 1935, W.E.B. Du Bois posed the question, "Does the Negro need separate schools?"[1] The question came as a result of Du Bois's assessment that the quality of education that African Americans were receiving in the nation's public schools was poor, an assessment that is still true today. Across the nation, a call in our urban centers for alternative schooling suggests that attempts to desegregate the public schools have ultimately not been beneficial to African American students. School systems in such cities as Milwaukee, Baltimore, Miami, Detroit, and New York are looking at experimental programs designed to meet the specific needs of African American boys.[2] The idea of special schools for African Americans (specifically African American boys) has sparked heated debate about both the ability and the responsibility of the public schools to educate adequately African American students. Why, in the 1990s, after decades of fighting for civil and equal rights, are African Americans even contemplating the possibility of separate schools?

The Current Climate

One look at the statistics provides some insight. African American students continue to lag significantly behind their white counterparts on all standard measures of achievement.[3] African

American children are three times as likely to drop out of school as white children are and twice as likely to be suspended from school.[4] The high school dropout rate in New York and California is about 35 percent; in inner cities, where large numbers of African Americans live, the rate nears 50 percent.[5] African American students make up only about 17 percent of the public school population but 41 percent of the special-education population.[6] These dismal statistics hold despite the two waves of educational reform initiated in the 1980s.[7]

These poor education statistics for African American students correlate with some harsh social and economic realities. Nearly one out of two African American children is poor. The rate of infant mortality among African Americans is twice that of whites. African American children are five times as likely as white children to be dependent on welfare and to become pregnant as teens; they are four times as likely to live with neither parent, three times as likely to live in a female-headed household, and twice as likely to live in substandard housing.[8] More young African American men are under the control of the criminal justice system than in college.[9] Indeed, an African American boy who was born in California in 1988 is three times more likely to be murdered than to be admitted to the University of California.[10]

These poor economic and social conditions have traditionally prompted African Americans to look to education, in the form of the integrated public school, as the most likely escape route to the American dream. In the landmark 1954 case *Brown vs. Board of Education*, Thurgood Marshall argued not only that the separate schools of the South were physically substandard but also that their very existence was psychologically damaging to African American children. Yet now, more than sixty years later, some African American educators and parents are asking themselves whether separate schools that put special emphases on the needs of their children might be the most expedient way to ensure that they receive a quality education.

While I was teaching in California, in the late 1980s, a reporter from another state called to ask my opinion about an African American male immersion school that was under consideration in her city.

"Correct me if I am wrong," I said, "but don't 90 percent of the African American students in your city already attend all-black schools?"

"Well, yes, I guess that's right," she responded. "So what you're really asking me is how I feel about single-sex schools?" I went on.

"No, that's not what I'm asking . . . I don't think," she said, with some doubt. "But now that you've reminded me that the schools really are already segregated, I guess I need to rethink my question."

The concern over African American immersion schools is not really about school segregation. Indeed, schools in large urban centers today are more segregated than ever before. Most African American children attend schools with other African American children. Further, as the whites and middle-income people of color (including African Americans, Latinos, and Asian Americans) fled the cities, they not only abandoned the schools to the poor children of color but also took with them the resources, by way of the diminishing tax base. In a better world I would want to see schools integrated across racial, cultural, linguistic, and all other lines. But I am too much of a pragmatist to ignore the sentiment and motivation underlying the African American immersion school movement. African Americans already have separate schools. The African American immersion school movement is about *taking control* of those separate schools.

I remember my first days in school. Despite the fact that there were close to thirty other five-year-olds vying for the attention of the one adult present, school seemed a lot like home. Everyone there was black. Several of my classmates were children I knew from my neighborhood. The teacher was an attractive, neatly dressed African American woman who told us how much fun we were each going to have and how much she expected us to learn. I thought school was a pretty neat place. It was safe and clean, with people who cared about you: again, a lot like home.

If one puts aside the obvious objections to separate schools that they are inequitable, undemocratic, regressive, and illegal and considers the possible merits, the current calls for separate schools may be understandable. First, most inner-city students already attend de facto segregated schools. At the time when a proposal was offered for the Milwaukee African American male schools, African American students in the Milwaukee public school system were already segregated in its inner-city schools. In fact, this proposal had been preceded by a call for the creation of a separate African American school district in Milwaukee.[11]

Second, the public schools have yet to demonstrate a sustained effort to provide quality education for African Americans. Despite modest gains in standardized test scores, the performance of African Americans in public schools, even those from relatively high-income stable families, remains behind that of whites from similar homes.

Third, some data suggest that African American children attending private and independent African American schools consistently perform at higher levels on standardized measures of achievement [than do those who attend public schools].[12] Of course, one might argue that students who attend private schools are a select subset of the school population and usually have supportive and involved parents, are more motivated, and have other economic and social advantages. However, a closer examination of the African American children who attend private schools reveals that large numbers of them are successful in these schools after having been unsuccessful in public schools.[13]

Historically, African Americans have wrestled with the problems of a quality education and integrated schooling. For some, a quality education does not necessarily mean attending schools with whites. As far back as the post–Civil War era there were African American champions of separate schools. At the constitutional convention of North Carolina, one African American delegate said: "I do not believe that it is good for our children to eat and drink daily the sentiment that they are naturally inferior to the whites. . . . I shall always do all that I can to have colored teachers for colored schools. This will necessitate separate schools as a matter of course, wherever possible, not by written law, but by mutual consent and the law of interest."[14]

However, not all African Americans believe that separate schools are the answer. In her study, Irvine found that many African Americans believe that resources and quality follow the white students.[15] When they look at the physical facilities and the instructional materials and other resources of middle-class white schools and compare them with inner-city schools, African American parents cannot help but surmise that where white children are there is educational excellence. Irvine found that middle-income African American parents who voluntarily sent their children to suburban white schools for purposes of desegregation routinely commented that these schools were of higher quality because they had more computers. Similarly, W.E.B. Du Bois initially felt that separate African American schools had little to offer: "The well-equipped Jim Crow school is a rare exception. For the most part, such schools have been run on wretchedly inadequate resources, taught by ignorant teachers; housed in huts and dumps; and given just as little attention and supervision as the authorities dared give them."[16]

But after witnessing the persistent mistreatment of African American students in desegregated Northern schools, Du Bois turned his efforts toward making the separate African American schools quality schools that offered equal education, not integrated education.

Certainly at the college level Fleming has demonstrated that African American students attending historically black colleges and universities (HBUCs) have significantly higher graduation rates than those attending predominately white institutions.[17] Further, the graduates' ability to function successfully both in the workplace and at predominately white graduate and professional schools is not compromised by their having attended African American undergraduate schools.

Indeed, some argue that school integration has come at considerable cost to African American students. Researchers investigating the performance of African American students in desegregated schools indicate that they fare no better than those attending segregated schools.[18] Lomotey and Staley suggest that school desegregation plans are deemed successful when white parents are satisfied, despite low academic performance and high suspension and dropout rates for African Americans.[19] The figures for African American males, in particular, are quite disturbing because of their overrepresentation in the suspension and dropout rates.

This assessment—that success of desegregation is determined by the white community's level of satisfaction—is consistent with a fictionalized account (based on actual reports of school desegregation) in law professor Derrick Bell's *And We Are Not Saved: The Elusive Quest for Racial Justice*.[20] In his discussion of the impact of school desegregation laws, Bell argues that the real beneficiaries of school desegregation are the schools, the white communities, and the white students. Desegregation often brings big dollars to a school district, which go toward instituting new programs, creating new jobs, providing transportation, and supporting staff development. Each of these means more personnel and better salaries. When white students are bused to African American schools, "desegregation money" is used to transform them into "magnet" schools—schools that attract students from throughout the district because they offer exemplary programs in mathematics, science, technology, the performing arts, and so on. Unfortunately, these magnet schools sometimes operate under a two-tiered system, virtually resegregating students within the so-called desegregated schools. Thus the white students who come to the schools benefit from the special program while the African American students remain in the low-level classes.

Lomotey and Staley report additional perks in the form of free extracurricular programs—such as after-school care, pre-school programs, and camping or skiing trips—to entice white students to attend these schools in African American and other nonwhite communities. These extras are open to all students, but the nature of these special enticements often makes them of less interest or importance for African American students. For example, few low income African American students have the resources or the equipment to enjoy camping or skiing.

McPartland[21] concluded that only when individual classrooms are desegregated is there an improvement in the achievement levels of African American students. This suggests that the classroom itself, where students come face to face with others who are different from themselves, is the place for real integration. When they are in the same classroom, all students can take advantage of the benefits and instructional expertise that may have been reserved previously for "upper-track" (that is, white middle-class) students.

Separate Schools or Special Schooling?

As a member of the baby boom generation, I went to urban schools that were bursting at the seams; every classroom had at least thirty students. Further, almost all of the children and most of the teachers were black. But the important thing was that the teachers were not strangers in the community. We students knew them and they knew us. We saw them at church, in the beauty parlor, in the grocery store. One of the sixth-grade teachers had served in the Army with my father. Most importantly, the teachers knew our families and had a sense of their dreams and aspirations for us.

Let us suppose that the legal, moral, and ethical concerns about special separate schools could either be suspended or reconciled with the American ideal of equality. Let us further suppose that every major urban center with a large number of African American students would set about developing separate schools for these children. One fundamental question would remain. Who would teach the children?

The uproar over separate schools has masked the debate about the quality and qualifications of the teachers who teach African American students. There is very little reliable literature on preparing teachers for diversity.[22] And almost nothing exists on teacher preparation specifically for African American students.[23]

Although the 1960s produced a large body of literature on teaching the "disadvantaged"[24] and the 1970s produced a body of literature about "effective schools,"[25] none of it was aimed specifically at preparing teachers to meet the needs of African American students. Even today some of the more popular educational innovations, such as cooperative learning and whole-language approaches to literacy, were developed and refined to improve achievement among "disadvantaged" students. Unfortunately, the relationship of these practices to African American learners is rarely made clear.

Elizabeth Cohen, a Stanford University sociologist, is one of the pioneers in the research of cooperative or small-group learning. Although her work in designing such classroom structures has received critical acclaim throughout the educational community, its link to her early work in facilitating school desegregation in Northern California is rarely acknowledged.[26]

When I searched the ERIC database for the years 1980 to 1990 using the descriptors "teacher education" and "black education," a mere twenty-seven cites emerged.[27] These cites included seven journal articles, ten conference papers, six reports, one book, and three teaching guides. Nine were based on empirical research.

Not one dealt specifically with preparing teachers to teach African American students.

One of the greatest hindrances to finding literature that addresses the needs of teachers of African American students is the language used to describe public school attempts to educate African Americans. As already mentioned, the literature of the 1960s and 1970s is filled with works about teaching the "culturally deprived[28] and disadvantaged."[29] Even when the goal was to improve both student and teacher effectiveness, the use of such terms contributed to a perception of African American students as deprived, deficient, and deviant. Because of this, many proposed educational interventions were designed to remove the students from their homes, communities, and cultures in an effort to mitigate against their alleged damaging effects.[30] Educational interventions, in the form of compensatory education (to compensate for the deprivation and disadvantage assumed to be inherent in African American homes and communities), often were based on a view of African American children as deficient white children.

When I was a child, Johnny Cromwell was one of the poorest children in our neighborhood. His parents worked hard at a number of menial jobs but there never seemed to be enough money to go around for him and his two sisters. He often showed up at school unkempt and unwashed. With the cruelty of children, we teased him and called him names. "Hey peasy head. Where'd you get them peas in your head? Is your father a farmer? He's gonna have a big ole crop of early June peas to pick, just pickin' at your head!" Although such teasing was very much a ritual of African American childhood, our teachers had a keen sense of when it hit too close to home. Regularly, Johnny was whisked into the teachers' room where his hair was combed, his face washed, and his disheveled clothes made more presentable. Our teachers understood the need to preserve the little dignity as a student that he had.

By the 1980s the language of deprivation had changed, but the negative connotations remained. According to Cuban, the term *at-risk* is now used to describe certain students and their families in much the same way that they had been described for almost two hundred years. Cuban further suggests that "the two most popular explanations for low academic achievement of at-risk children locate the problem in the children themselves or in their families."[31] Even the Educational Index continues to cross-reference African American student issues with the phrase "culturally deprived."

Given the long history of the poor academic performance of African American students one might ask why almost no literature exists to address their specific educational needs. One reason is a stubborn refusal in American education to recognize African Americans as a distinct cultural group. While it is recognized that African Americans make up a distinct *racial* group, the acknowledgment that this racial group has a distinct *culture* is still not recognized. It is presumed that African American children are exactly like white children but just need a little extra help. Rarely investigated are the possibilities of distinct cultural characteristics (requiring some specific attention) or the detrimental impact of systemic racism. Thus the reasons for their academic failure continue to be seen as wholly environmental and social. Poverty and lack of opportunity often are presented as the only plausible reasons for poor performance. And the kinds of interventions and remedies proposed attempt to compensate for these deficiencies.

"When you sing in our school choir, you sing as proud Negro children" boomed the voice of Mrs. Benn, my fifth-grade teacher. *"Don't you know that Marian Anderson, a cultured colored woman, is the finest contralto ever? Haven't you ever heard Paul Robeson sing? It can just take your breath away. We are not shiftless and lazy folk. We are hard-working, God-fearing people. You can't sing in this choir unless you want to hold up the good name of our people."*

It never occurred to me in those days that African Americans were not a special people. My education both at home and at school reinforced that idea. We were a people who overcame incredible odds.

I knew that we were discriminated against but I witnessed too much competence—and excellence—to believe that African Americans didn't have distinctly valuable attributes.

Hollins has looked carefully at programs and strategies that have demonstrated a level of effectiveness with African American students.[32] Her examination suggests that these programs fall into three broad categories—those designed to remediate or accelerate without attending to the students' social or cultural needs; those designed to resocialize African American students to mainstream behaviors, values, and attitudes at the same time that they teach basic skills; and those designed to facilitate student learning by capitalizing on the students' own social and cultural backgrounds.

Falling within the first category are programs like the Chicago Mastery Learning Reading Program, where the focus is on remediation or acceleration in the basic skills.[33] Hollins suggests that such programs, while they pay close attention to pacing, monitoring of instruction, and precise sequencing of objectives, virtually ignore the social or cultural needs of students.

The widely publicized New Haven, Connecticut, program entitled "A Social Skills Curriculum for Inner-City Children" is an example of a program that fits into Hollins's second category.[34] This program represents an explicit attempt "to resocialize youngsters viewed as outside the mainstream and to inculcate in them mainstream perceptions and behaviors."[35] The philosophy behind such programs resembles that of the compensatory educational models of the 1960s and 1970s in that the children's academic problems are seen to be rooted in the "pathology" of their homes, communities, and cultures. Thus if the children can be removed or isolated from their culture of "deprivation" then the school can transform them into people worthy of inclusion in the society.

Programs in the third category attempt to capitalize on students' individual, group, and cultural differences. Rather than ignoring or minimizing cultural differences, these programs see the differences as strengths to base academic achievement on. Cummins suggests that students are less likely to fail in school settings where they feel positive about both their own culture and the majority culture and "are not alienated from their own cultural values."[36] The work of Au and Jordan in Hawaii is an example of teachers' use of the students' own culture to improve their reading performance.[37] Hollins argues that Chicago's Westside Preparatory School is an example of a program that uses African American culture to improve the students' academic performance.[38]

Even putting these programs with underlying agendas to resocialize African American students aside, there is some evidence to suggest more generally that when African American students attempt to achieve in school they do so at a psychic cost.[39] Somehow many have come to equate exemplary performance in school with a loss of their African American identity; that is, doing well in school is seen as "acting white." Thus if they do not want to "act white," the only option, many believe, is to refuse to do well in school.[40] Thus they purposely learn how not to learn. In contrast, the opportunity to be excellent academically, socially, and culturally underlies the thinking in many African American immersion schools.[41] When schools support their culture as an integral part of the school experience, students can understand that academic excellence is not the sole province of white middle-class students. Such systems also negate the axiomatic thinking that if doing well in school equals "acting white" then doing poorly equals "acting black."

I was sent to an integrated junior high school that was not in my neighborhood. I describe it as "integrated" rather than "desegregated" because no court mandates placed black children there. I was there because my mother was concerned about the quality of our neighborhood school.

There were a handful of African American students in my seventh-grade class, but I knew none of them. They lived in a more affluent neighborhood than I did. Their parents had stable blue collar or white collar jobs. They had gone to better-equipped elementary schools than I had. The white students were even more privileged. Their fathers had impressive jobs as doctors, lawyers—one was a photojournalist. Most of their mothers were homemakers. In contrast, my mother and father both worked full-time. My father often even worked two jobs, yet we still lived more modestly than most of my classmates did.

In seventh grade I learned what it means to be competitive. In elementary school my teachers did not seem to make a big deal out of my academic achievements. They encouraged me but did not hold me up as an example that might intimidate slower students. Although I suspect I was a recipient of a kind of sponsored mobility—perhaps because my mother always sent me to school neat and clean and with my hair combed—I don't think this preferential treatment was obvious to other students. But in my new surroundings the competition was very obvious. Many of my white classmates made a point of showing off their academic skills. Further, their parents actively lent a hand in important class assignments and projects. For example, one boy had horrible penmanship. You could barely read what he scrawled in class, but he always brought in neatly typed homework. I asked him once if he did the typing and he told me that his mother typed everything for him. She also did the typing for his cousin, who was also in our class and had beautiful penmanship. The teachers often commented on the high quality of these typed papers.

I had come from a school where children learned and produced together. This competitiveness, further encouraged by the parents, was new to me. I could attempt to keep up with this unfair competition and "act white" or I could continue to work my hardest and hope that I could still achieve.

A Study of Effective Teaching for African Americans

This book examines effective teaching for African American students and how such teaching has helped students not only achieve academic success but also achieve that success while maintaining a positive identity as African Americans. It is about the kind of teaching that promotes this excellence despite little administrative or collegial support. It is about the kind of teaching that the African American community has identified as having its children's best interests at heart. It is about the kind of teaching that helps students *choose* academic success.

This book is based on my study of successful teachers of African American students, which was funded by a 1988 postdoctoral grant from the National Academy of Education's Spencer Foundation. I conducted this research during the 1988–89 and 1989–90 school years, with an additional in-depth study of two classrooms in the 1990–91 school year. The opinions expressed in this publication do not necessarily reflect the position, policy, or endorsement of the National Academy of Education or of the Spencer Foundation.

I make a distinction between *excellent teaching* and *excellent teachers* purposely. Although each of the teachers who participated in my study are superb individually, this book looks at a teaching ideology and common behaviors, not at individual teaching styles. By choosing this path, I lose some of the distinctive and rich personal qualities of these marvelous individuals. However, I sacrifice this richness in favor of a focus on "the art and craft of teaching."[42] This focus is important because it minimizes the tendency to reduce the research findings to individual idiosyncrasies and to suggest a "cult-of-personality" explanation for effective teaching. Looking carefully at the teaching, while offering the teachers as exemplars, provides a useful heuristic for teachers and teacher educators who wish to take on the challenge of being successful with African American students.

This book is about teaching practice, not about curriculum. Much of the purported reforms and the debate about our schools focuses on curriculum: What should we teach? Whose version of history should we offer? What priority should different subject matters be given? But it is *the way we teach* that profoundly affects the way that students perceive the content of that curriculum.

My notions in this domain are strongly aligned with Giroux and Simon's thoughts on critical pedagogy:

> Pedagogy refers to a deliberate attempt to influence how and what knowledge and identities are produced within and among particular sets of social relations. It can be understood as a practice through which people are incited to acquire a particular "moral character." As both a political and practical activity, it attempts to influence the occurrence and qualities of experiences. When one practices pedagogy, one acts with the intent of creating experiences that will organize and disorganize a variety of understandings of our natural and social world in particular ways. . . . Pedagogy is a concept which draws attention to the processes through which knowledge is produced.[43]

Because of this pedagogical view, I went into the classrooms intending to examine both "the political and the practical." I wanted to see not only why a certain kind of teaching helped the students to be more successful academically but also how this kind of teaching supported and encouraged students to use their prior knowledge to make sense of the world and to work toward improving it.

In the next chapter, I begin to examine the concept of culturally relevant teaching and how it can improve the educational lives of African American students. As is true of most researchers, it is my hope that this research will find broad applicability and be seen as useful for teaching students of any race or ethnicity.

* 2 *

Does Culture Matter?

But when they returned to their own land, they didn't go through Jerusalem . . . for God had warned them in a dream to go home another way.

—MATTHEW 2:12

At first glance, the quote from the Bible that opens this chapter may seem out of place. The passage refers to the three wise men, who were instructed by King Herod to return to him after they had visited the Messiah. Herod supposedly wanted to know the whereabouts of the Baby Jesus so that he, too, could go and worship him. But the wise men were warned in a dream to take a different route home for if Herod knew of Jesus' whereabouts he would surely have had him killed.

The analogy that I am making here is that the pedagogical instruction that many teachers of African American students received—from their teacher preparation programs, from their administrators, and from "conventional wisdom"—leads to an intellectual death. Thus successful teachers, like the wise men of the Bible, travel a different route to ensure the growth and development of their students.

Over the past ten years there has been increased interest in looking at ways to improve the academic performance of students who are culturally, ethnically, racially, and linguistically diverse.

Mohatt and Erickson investigated classroom interactions, specifically the differences in interactions between Native American students and their white and Native American teachers.[1] The study revealed that the teachers who were most

17

effective in communicating with the students used an interactional style that the authors termed "culturally congruent." This
notion of cultural congruence is meant to signify the ways in
which the teachers altered their speech patterns, communication styles, and participation structures to resemble more closely
those of the students' own culture.

Au and Jordan used the term "cultural appropriateness" to
describe the methods teachers used to work with native Hawaiian
students to improve their reading performance.[2] Rather than
teach them to read by using phonics, the teachers arranged the
students in small groups and emphasized reading comprehension
rather than word decoding. The students were encouraged to discuss what they read in a style similar to their at-home communication style: an overlapping interactional style (which might
be seen in some cultures as interrupting) that resembled what is
known in native Hawaiian culture as "talk story."

Other studies have looked at "cultural responsiveness"[3] and
"cultural compatibility."[4] Like the notion of cultural appropriateness, these terms are in a sociolinguistic lexicon used to analyze
the ways in which schools can be made more accessible to culturally diverse learners. But in a challenge to the sociolinguistic
perspective, Villegas suggests that the difficulties that students
of color experience in school are far more complex than "differences between the language and culture of home and school."[5]
Villegas maintains that culturally diverse students' failure in
school results from societal conflict and a struggle for power.
This view is consistent with the work of such critical theorists as
Giroux[6] and McLaren.[7]

However, although some African American scholars have
argued that they are in agreement with the critical theorists
about schools as a battleground in the struggle for power and the
exercise of authority, the failure of these theorists to examine
adequately the special historical, social, economic, and political
role that race plays in the United States makes their argument

less than complete for improving the educational lives of African Americans.[8]

Recently African American scholars have begun to look at specific cultural strengths of African American students and the ways that some teachers leverage these strengths effectively to enhance academic and social achievement. Scholars like Hale-Benson[9] and Taylor and Dorsey-Gaines[10] have identified cultural strengths that African American children bring with them to the classroom that are rarely capitalized on by teachers. For example, even white scholars who have looked carefully at language communities suggest that schools place little value on what is termed the "nonstandard English" that African American children bring to school even though that language is rich, diverse, and useful in both community and work settings.[11]

Irvine has suggested that what happens between African American students and their teachers represents a lack of "cultural synchronization."[12] She further suggests that this lack of cultural synchronization and responsiveness relates to other factors that inhibit African American students' school achievement, including the "prescriptive ideologies and prescriptive structures that are premised on normative belief systems."[13]

The Notion of Cultural Relevance

The notion of "cultural relevance" moves beyond language to include other aspects of student and school culture.[14] Thus culturally relevant teaching uses student culture in order to maintain it and to transcend the negative effects of the dominant culture. The negative effects are brought about, for example, by not seeing one's history, culture, or background represented in the textbook or curriculum or by seeing that history, culture, or background distorted. Or they may result from the staffing pattern in the school (when all teachers and the principal are white and only the janitors and cafeteria workers are African American, for example) and from the tracking of African American students into the lowest-level classes. The primary aim of culturally relevant teaching is to assist in the development of a "relevant black personality" that allows African American students to choose academic excellence yet still identify with African and African American culture.[15]

Specifically, culturally relevant teaching is a pedagogy that empowers students intellectually, socially, emotionally, and politically by using cultural referents to impart knowledge, skills, and attitudes. These cultural referents are not merely vehicles for bridging or explaining the dominant culture; they are aspects of the curriculum in their own right. For example, let us examine how a fifth-grade teacher might use a culturally relevant style in a lesson about the U.S. Constitution. She might begin with a discussion of the bylaws and articles of incorporation that were used to organize a local church or African American civic association. Thus the students learn the significance of such documents in forming institutions and shaping ideals while they also learn that their own people are institution-builders. This kind of moving between the two cultures lays the foundation for a skill that the students will need in order to reach academic and cultural success.

How Teachers See African American Students

In fifth grade I met the teacher who I think is most responsible for my belief that some teachers truly motivate students to be their very best. This was Mrs. Benn. At first, I didn't want her as my teacher. She was an African American woman and she was old: in her late 50s. She was also heavyset and had large breasts. She wore flowered dresses and the black shoes we called "old lady comforters"; they looked like orthopedic shoes. On her legs she wore cotton support stockings. Her thinning hair was pulled back into a bun with a fine hair net around it. She wore what were later fashionably termed granny glasses but they were not fashionable at that time. The other fifth-grade teacher was the young, white, vibrant Miss Plunkett. Miss Plunkett had long brown hair, which she wore in a ponytail that bounced attractively when she walked. She smiled a lot; she almost looked like a prototype for a Barbie doll. She seemed an infinitely more desirable teacher than old Mrs. Benn.

But it took only a short time for me to discover that I had been wrong about Mrs. Benn. The wife of a Baptist minister, she approached her teaching with a missionary-like zeal. There was no aspect of working with children that seemed boring or routine to Mrs. Benn. She was generous to a fault. When I begrudgingly asked her to purchase Girl Scout cookies from me she lamented the fact that I had waited so long. She had already bought cookies from another student, she said, so she could only buy a few from me. She bought eleven boxes!

Mrs. Benn was the director of the school chorus and she expected every student in her class to be in it. It did not matter how weakly you croaked along—as Mrs. Benn's student you sang in the chorus. She took the chorus all around the city; she featured us in churches where her husband was the guest speaker.

Mrs. Benn also took us to her home. And she instilled in us a sense of responsibility by requiring us to take home the classroom plants on weekends or long vacations. She expected those plants to come back thriving—and they did. She was a proud woman who demanded excellence at every task we undertook. We were required to write with precise handwriting and perfect spelling. She taught every subject—from reading to physical education—and she warned us that playing around in her class meant that we did not value ourselves. "This is your chance, don't let it slip away," she urged.

I cannot remember Mrs. Benn ever sending a student to the principal's office. If you misbehaved in her class, you had to sit in the cramped leg opening of her desk—then she sat down at the desk and pulled her chair in close. I never had the displeasure of having to sit in that opening, but I was able to imagine the horrible experience: nothing *to look at but the three sides of the wooden desk and the cotton-stockinged, heavy old legs of a woman who could easily be your grand-mother.*

Most importantly for me, Mrs. Benn opened up the world of U.S. history. She told glorious tales of exploration and invention. She was a great storyteller and, unlike any teacher I had ever known before, she made a point of telling us about what "the colored folks" contributed to this story.

Imagine yourself in a kindergarten classroom. The teacher, an older white woman, is attempting to conduct a discussion with a very active group of five- and six-year-olds who are gathered together on a square of carpeting in one corner of the room. As the teacher attempts to discuss a story she has read them, various children talk to their neighbors, hop up from their seats, and move to different areas of the room. No one particular student or group of students is participating in this kind of behavior more than another. However, over the course of a thirty-minute period, the only children who are verbally reprimanded for their behavior are the three African Americans. Asian American children who engage in identical behaviors are never spoken to. What is happening in this classroom?

Imagine another situation. An eager student teacher from the local university is at an introductory meeting with her cooperating teacher. The meeting takes place in the teachers' lounge where other teachers in the school are able to hear everything said. At one point in the discussion the cooperating teacher, who is regarded as one of the district's finest, tells the student teacher that she will have to be especially careful to recognize that there are two types of black students in the school. She observes that there are "white-blacks" and "black-blacks." The white-blacks are easy to deal with because they come from "good" homes and have "white" values. But the black-blacks are less capable academically and have behavior problems. As the student teacher listens she is shocked by what her cooperating teacher is saying but she is even more shocked that none of the other teachers in the lounge appears to find what's being said unusual. What is happening here?

Imagine one final situation. A student teacher who has volunteered to participate in a special group of student teachers who are interested in teaching in diverse settings is talking in the student teaching practicum seminar. She tells the group about her inconsistent disciplinary methods. When the white children in her class misbehave she sternly reprimands them because, she believes, they know the rules and they know what they are supposed to do. However, when the seven African American students misbehave, she gives them another chance. In her own words, she allows them to "get away with murder" because she feels sorry for them and wants them to know that she "cares." What is happening with this teacher?

Each of these "imagined" stories actually is true.[16] The answers to the questions posed at the end of each are very important because they explain how teachers often see African American students. These are not "bad" teachers. These very same people decry racism; they believe in equal opportunity. However, they do not understand that their perceptions of African American students interfere with their ability to be effective teachers for them.

The significance of teacher expectations on student achievement has been examined in many studies.[17] Winfield has suggested that a teacher's beliefs about inner-city students can be categorized along four dimensions: seeking improvement versus doing maintenance and assuming responsibility versus shifting responsibility (see Figure 2.1).[18] Winfield's cross-classification system yields four possible teacher behavior patterns—they can be tutors, general contractors, custodians, or referral agents. *Tutors* believe that students can improve and they believe it is their responsibility to help them do so. *General contractors* also believe that improvement is possible, but they look for ancillary personnel (aides, resource teachers, and so on) to provide

Figure 2.1. Behaviors Toward Academically At-Risk Students.

		Assume Responsibility	Shift Responsibility
Beliefs About Academically At-Risk Students	Seek Improvement	(1) Tutors	(2) General Contractors
	Maintain the Status Quo	(3) Custodians	(4) Referral Agents

Source: Reprinted with permission from L. Winfield, "Teacher Beliefs Toward Academically At-Risk Students in Inner Urban Schools," *The Urban Review*, 1986, 18(4), 253–267.

academic assistance rather than take on the responsibility themselves. *Custodians* do not believe that much can be done to help their students but they do not look for others to help them maintain the students at these low levels. *Referral agents* do not believe that much can be done to help their students improve either, but they shift the responsibility [for maintaining students at these low levels] to other school personnel, by sending them off to the school psychologist or the special education teacher. One perspective on these low expectations and negative beliefs about African American students comes from mainstream society's invalidation of African American culture.[19] This invalidation of African American culture is compounded by a notion of assimilationist teaching, a teaching style that operates without regard to the students' particular cultural characteristics. According to the assimilationist perspective, the teacher's role is to ensure that students fit into society. And if the teacher has low expectations, the place that the teacher believes the students "fit into" is on society's lower rungs.

If we return to the classroom situations described earlier, we can analyze the effects of teacher expectations and assimilationist perspectives. In the first situation, the kindergarten teacher has internalized a notion that African American students must be controlled in order to be taught. Because she expects the African American students to be harder to control she works harder to control them. When the Asian American students exhibit the same behaviors, she ignores them. The teacher is engaging in assimilationist teaching behaviors because she has developed societal categories in her mind that the students fit into. Her attitude to the students not only tells them what she believes about them but also tells all the other students in the class what they should believe about them.

In the second situation, the teacher has made a distinction between two groups of African American students based on social class. It is clear that she does not honor the students of either class. The denigration of the lower-income students is obvious but her perception of "goodness" in the middle-income African American students is merely tied to her vision of how closely their behaviors and mannerisms match what she sees as white attributes. Thus her expectations for all the children are based on racist notions and, furthermore, they go unchallenged by her colleagues.

In the third situation the teacher, who on the surface may appear to be acting in the exact opposite way from the first, also demonstrates low expectations for the African American students. She does not demand excellence from them because she believes them to be incapable of meeting rigorous standards of behavior, and so her response is sympathy. She gives little thought to how her low expectations impede the students' progress. Culturally relevant teaching is the antithesis of the assimilationist teaching typified in all of these examples. Culturally relevant teaching may be depicted by another version of Winfield's conceptualization. Rather than aiming for slight improvement or maintenance, culturally relevant teaching aims at another

Figure 2.2. Behaviors Toward Academically and Culturally At-Risk Students.

	Assume Responsibility	Share/Shift Responsibility
Seek Excellence	(1) Conductors	(2) Coaches
Seek Improvement	(3) Tutors	(4) General Contractors
Maintain the Status Quo	(5) Custodians	(6) Referral Agents

Beliefs About At-Risk Students

level—excellence—and transforms shifting responsibility into *sharing* responsibility (see Figure 2.2). As they strive for excellence, such teachers function as *conductors* or *coaches*. *Conductors* believe that students are capable of excellence and they assume responsibility for ensuring that their students achieve that excellence. If we push the metaphor we can visualize an orchestra conductor who approaches the orchestra stand; all members of the orchestra have their eyes fixed on the conductor. Nothing happens without the conductor's direction. So powerful can be the personality of the conductor be that the audience and musical critics describe the quality of the performance in terms of the conductor's performance, even though the conductor did not play a single note.

Two of the teachers who participated in my study can be described as conductors. Their personal charisma and sense of drama were catalysts that helped propel students to academic excellence.

Much like the well-known Marva Collins of Chicago and Jaime Escalante of Los Angeles, these teachers exuded special personal qualities over which they lay their pedagogical skills. At my university, I was lucky enough to have this kind of teacher, too:

"Don't take Dr. Jones's humanities course," several students at my historically black university urged. "She'll work you to death, plus she's crazy!" But unable to find another humanities section to fit my schedule, I found myself in the dreaded Dr. Jones's class. And my classmates were right. She was demanding—there were volumes of reading and tests every week. And she was crazy! She dressed in black from head to toe. Her makeup looked as if it had been applied by Count Dracula. She seemed to be able to stare a hole through you with her dark-ringed eyes. And every class was a performance. Yet once I got over my fear of this woman I found that I sat with my eyes riveted on her. I never wasted time in small talk with the other students during her class. And I never missed a class. I could not recall ever learning so much from one person. She seemed to know everything. And everybody in the class seemed spellbound—even the football player who sat to my left taking furious notes. At the end of every hour we all looked at each other and said, "Wow!"

Like the conductors, coaches also believe their students are capable of excellence, but they are comfortable sharing the responsibility to help them achieve it with parents, community members, and the students themselves. Most of the teachers who participated in my study can be described as coaches. Here again, an elaboration of the coaching metaphor is helpful in explaining how they operate in the classroom.

Coaches understand that the goal is team success. They know that they do not need to gain personal recognition in order to achieve that success. However, they do need a sense of how to blend the talents of the players to form a winning team. Coaches are comfortable operating behind the scenes and on the sidelines. The players are always mindful of the coach's expectations but they know that even the best game plan will fail without proper execution. The players understand that they work together with the coach to achieve the goal.

My sixth-grade teacher was a coach. She could yell, scream, cajole, and nag with the best of them. But we knew that the constant pushing was for our benefit. "You know you can do better," was her favorite phrase. We laughed about her repeating it so often. On the playground and in our neighborhoods we would tease each other when we were not successful at stickball or double Dutch. "You know you can do better," we would sing and quickly dissolve into laughter. Funny, the sound of her voice repeating that phrase haunted me as a college student, as a graduate student, and as a university professor: "You know you can do better!"

Teachers who practice culturally relevant methods can be identified by the way they see themselves and others. They see their teaching as an art rather than as a technical skill. They believe that all of their students can succeed rather than that failure is inevitable for some. They see themselves as a part of the community and they see teaching as giving back to the community. They help students make connections between their local, national, racial, cultural, and global identities. Such teachers can also be identified by the ways in which they structure their social interactions: Their relationships with students are fluid and equitable and extend beyond the classroom. They demonstrate a connectedness with all of their students and encourage that same connectedness between the students. They encourage a community of learners; they encourage their students to learn collaboratively. Finally, such teachers are identified by their notions of knowledge: They believe that knowledge is continuously re-created, recycled, and shared by teachers and students alike. They view the content of the curriculum critically and are passionate about it. Rather than expecting students to demonstrate prior knowledge and skills they help students develop that knowledge by building bridges and scaffolding for learning.

In the subsequent chapters of this book, these qualities—how such teachers see themselves and others, how they structure social interactions, and how they conceive of knowledge—will be explored in-depth through examples of the teaching behaviors that typify these qualities. Because these behaviors are examined in context, they intersect and overlap. I use these categories or dimensions as conceptual rubrics with which to simplify complex pedagogical beliefs and behaviors.

These explorations take the form of pedagogical cases. Shulman[20] points out that a case is not merely a narrative account of an event. It is an example of a larger class of events (for example, a case of classroom management, a case of reading instruction). In this book, rather than detail how each individual teacher exemplifies a specific characteristic, I use a varied narrative to illustrate culturally relevant teaching practices. Thus instead of offering mere advice, I attempt to provide examples of culturally relevant teaching in specific contexts. I have taken this approach because I believe in a broad definition of pedagogy; in other words, even when teachers carry out seemingly noninstructional actions, such as smiling at a student or showing disapproval of a student, they are engaged in pedagogy.

This book attempts to look at pedagogy holistically and to demonstrate that culturally relevant teaching is not a series of steps that teachers can follow or a recipe for being effective with African American students. Although I provide explanations and derivations as a researcher, I recognize that teachers and other readers bring their own perspectives to this text. Therefore, I anticipate that they will suggest other interpretations and explanations because of their own pedagogical situations and contexts.

A Group Profile of the Teachers Who Participated in the Study

I remember every teacher I ever had. I say this not to boast about my memory but to illustrate just how powerfully my teachers influenced me.

Some of them I knew quite well, particularly those in the elementary school, because of the intense relationship between elementary school teachers and their students in their self-contained classrooms and because they lived in my community and were a part of my life outside the classroom. Others I knew only as teachers. I had no idea what their lives were like outside the school, or even if they had lives outside of school. The story of those I knew well could be the subject of a book unto itself. Memories of the others provoke a series of questions for me. Who were you really? What did you care about? What did you think of me? Did you even know who I was?

Although in the remainder of the book I will examine specific examples of culturally relevant teaching, it is appropriate here to profile briefly the group of individuals I studied. This was a small-scale, ethnographic study that included only eight teachers.

Unlike more traditional studies, my study did not use so-called objective measures to identify teacher proficiency. Thus students' standardized test scores alone were not considered an indicator of "good teaching." Instead, I approached the educational "consumers"—parents. They were solicited for their insights into good teaching. In essence, I asked them to identify the teachers who met the educational standards that they felt were important. These parents indicated that they had a dual agenda for those they considered good teachers. They wanted them to help their children succeed at traditional academic tasks (reading, writing, mathematics, and so on), but at the same time they wanted them to provide an education that would not alienate their children from their homes, their community, and their culture. One parent verbalized this as wanting their children to be able to "hold their own in the classroom without forgetting their own in the community."[21] Using the dual goal for both academic and cultural excellence, the parents generated a list of more than twenty teachers they felt passed the test.

Second, I met with principals of the various schools to see if they could suggest teachers who they felt demonstrated effectiveness with African American students. The principals identified what might appear to be more conventional criteria by which to judge effective teachers. They cited test scores, classroom management and student discipline, and student attendance and satisfaction. The principals also generated a list of more than twenty potential candidates.

The sample I used included teachers who appeared on both the parents' and principals' lists. There were a total of nine teachers; all but one agreed to participate in the study.

In an earlier paper I characterized my description of these eight teachers as a "snapshot."[22] I felt this was an appropriate metaphor because it describes a brief, candid glimpse. Unlike "portraits," where the subject is posed to appear in the best light and where elements that are less than perfect are retouched, my snapshots "are rough and unfinished"—little slices of teachers' lives at specific points in time.[23] Here is a snapshot overview.

Five African American teachers and three white teachers were included in the study. All women, they ranged in teaching experience from twelve to forty years. They had taught in a variety of schools including rural white and African American, suburban white, suburban integrated, and private and public urban African American schools. Three had attended historically black colleges; three predominately white state colleges. One had attended a predominately white Catholic college and one a normal school.

For the purposes of this study, I assigned each teacher a "culture of reference." This term refers to the cultural group (including ethnic and racial characteristics) that the teacher most closely identified with. Who were her friends inside and outside the school? What kinds of social activities did she participate in and which neighborhoods and communities did she frequent?

All the African American teachers had an African American culture of reference. Their friends and associates outside the school were predominately African Americans. Those who were church members attended African American churches. Those who were members of established social organizations (such as clubs or sororities) belonged to African American groups. Three of them lived in the predominately African American, Latino, and Pacific Islander community of the school district. Of the white teachers, one had a white culture of reference. She lived in a white community and had few African American contacts outside of the school.[24] Another had what may be called a bicultural orientation. She had a relatively equal number of white and African American friends and often hosted social gatherings that included both groups. She listed among her most intimate friends both African Americans and whites. After a family tragedy she elected to stay with an African American who was a long-time friend and traveling companion during the grieving process. Interestingly, the third white teacher had an African American culture of reference. Her friends and social contacts outside of school were almost exclusively African American. She was conversant in African American dialect and was sometimes mistaken over the phone for an African American. She had lived in the local community her entire life. She and one of the African American teachers went to school together in that district.

In the subsequent chapters, I will introduce each teacher individually as I attempt to explain aspects of her pedagogy and her beliefs about teaching. To maintain privacy and anonymity, I use pseudonyms rather than the teachers' real names.

Because of the in-depth nature of the study and the three years that I spent with these teachers, this book reflects more than surface knowledge of them and their pedagogy. But once again I stress my hope that retelling their collective stories will illustrate their culturally relevant teaching and not their personal idiosyncrasies. Rather than show how different they are as individuals, I intend to pull together the commonalities in their philosophy, pedagogy, and personal commitment.

* 3 *

Seeing Color,
Seeing Culture

*I have a dream that my four children will one day live in a
nation where they will not be judged by the color of their skin
but by the content of their character.*

—MARTIN LUTHER KING JR., AUGUST 28, 1963

*I*n second grade my classmates and I all read from the same Dick
and Jane basal reader. I was chastised more than once for reading ahead. But during that year I was also chosen to attend a special
reading class. Unlike today's remedial reading classes, that class was
reserved for accelerated readers. We were a select group of about five
or six students and we went to reading class each day for about thirty to
forty minutes. There we read "real" books, not basal textbooks, about
faraway places and interesting people.

Our teacher was Mrs. Gray, a tall, elegant African American
woman who seemed to love children and the idea that she could expose
them to new experiences. One Saturday just before Christmas break
Mrs. Gray took the class downtown on the subway train to see the
dancing fountains and the Christmas display at John Wanamaker's,
Philadelphia's landmark department store. I had been in Wanamaker's
many times to shop with my mother, but this was the first time I could
remember being taken for the express purpose of being entertained.
"Now remember," admonished Mrs. Gray, "when we get downtown
people will be looking at us. If you misbehave they're not going to
say, look at those bad children. They're going to say look at those bad
colored children!" She did not have to tell us twice. We knew that we

33

*were held to a higher standard than other people. We knew that people
would stare at us and that the stares would come because of our skin
color. Despite the "burden of blackness," it was a magical visit. I felt
special. I felt important. I felt smart!*

The Basics of Culturally Relevant Teaching

In this chapter I discuss the ways that the teachers in my study
see themselves, their students, and their students' parents. With
each vignette I attempt to introduce the teachers individually
and to share information about them—by way of interview comments and classroom observations—that illustrates their culturally relevant practices. Rather than attempt to show how all of
the teachers demonstrate culturally relevant teaching in all of its
aspects, I have selected examples that I believe are most illustra-
tive of each aspect.

First, let us begin with a look at the many teachers who are
reluctant to acknowledge racial differences or grapple with these
and other differences in the classroom.

In her book *White Teacher*, Paley suggested that teachers must
take care not to ignore color.[1] When she moved to an integrated
private school, an African American parent confronted her with
the "knowledge" that her children were black and knew they
were black, and she wanted that difference to be recognized as
a comfortable and natural one. Delpit's review of Paley's book
points to this as the beginning of "the journey toward acknowledging and valuing differences."[2]

My own experiences with white teachers, both preservice and
veteran, indicate that many are uncomfortable acknowledging
any student differences and particularly racial differences. Thus
some teachers make such statements as "I don't really see color,
I just see children" or "I don't care if they're red, green, or polka
dot, I just treat them all like children." However, these attempts

at color-blindness mask a "dysconscious racism," an "uncritical habit of mind that justifies inequity and exploitation by accepting the existing order of things as given."[3] This is not to suggest that these teachers are racist in the conventional sense. They do not consciously deprive or punish African American children on the basis of their race, but at the same time they are not unconscious of the ways in which some children are privileged and others are disadvantaged in the classroom. Their "dysconsciousness" comes into play when they fail to challenge the status quo, when they accept the given as the inevitable.

In an earlier study that illustrated this kind of behavior, preservice teachers were asked to explain the economic, social, and educational disparities that exist between white and African American children.[4] Presented with data on African American and white children's life chances, the students were asked three questions: How can you explain these disparities? What are some differing ideological explanations for these disparities? What can schools do about these disparities?

The students' responses to the first question provide some telling insights. Most cited the fact that African Americans had been enslaved as the explanation for their present economic, social, and educational conditions. A few students suggested that African Americans' failure to gain equal opportunities in the society explained the disparities. Only one student offered racism as an explanation.

The belief of the majority of the students—that African Americans' enslavement more than a hundred years ago explains today's disparities—suggests that they could not envision how conditions could be otherwise. The enslavement of African Americans is a part of history. Thus, according to this view, the past alone determines the future of a people. A more fundamental problem with this point of view in the classroom context is the following: If a teacher looks out at a classroom and sees the sons and daughters of slaves, how does that vision translate into her expectations for educational excellence? How can teachers who see African American students as mere descendants of slaves be expected to inspire them to educational, economic, and social levels that may even exceed their own?

The usual antidote for this persistent view of African American children is for the viewer to pretend that he or she does not see the color that once forced their ancestors into slavery. Thus the teacher claims to be color-blind. However, such claims cannot be valid. Given the significance of race and color in American society, it is impossible to believe that a classroom teacher does not notice the race and ethnicity of the children she is teaching. Further, by claiming not to notice, the teacher is saying that she is dismissing one of the most salient features of the child's identity and that she does not account for it in her curricular planning and instruction. Saying we are aware of students' race and ethnic background is not the same as saying we treat students inequitably. The passion for equality in the American ethos has many teachers (and others) equating equality with sameness. An example may further clarify this point.

In a classroom of thirty children a teacher has one student who is visually impaired, one who is wheelchair-bound, one who has limited English proficiency, and one who is intellectually gifted. If the teacher presents identical work in identical ways to all of the students, is she dealing equitably or inequitably with the children? The visually impaired student cannot read the small print on an assignment, the wheelchair-bound student cannot do push-ups in gym, the foreign-language student cannot give an oral report in English, and the intellectually gifted student learns nothing by spelling words she mastered several years ago.

The notion of equity as sameness only makes sense when all students *are* exactly the same. But even within the nuclear family children born from the same parents are not exactly the same. Different children have different needs and addressing those different needs is the best way to deal with them equitably. The same is true in the classroom. If teachers pretend not to see students' racial and ethnic differences, they really do not see the students at all and are limited in their ability to meet their educational needs.

Teachers with Culturally Relevant Practices Have High Self-Esteem and a High Regard for Others

Although my neighborhood was predominately African American, a few white families lived there. Most attended Catholic schools. It made sense to us; they were Catholic. One of the neighborhood white boys went to a private boarding school. His father had died, and this made him eligible for a private school for orphan boys (I guess a mother's presence did not count in those days). The school he attended did not accept African American boys. (Many years later that school would become a battleground in the civil rights struggle in our city.) Only one white family, which consisted of seventeen children, sent their kids to my elementary school. They were extremely poor and often showed up unclean and unkempt. Everyone in the school community knew them and some felt a pang of sympathy for them, for as poor as we all were, we knew we were not quite as poor as they were.

But they seemed to take some comfort in the fact that although they were extremely poor at least they were not black. Every fight these children ever had came as a result of their calling one of the African American children "nigger." We had to wonder who or what they thought we were. And what did that make them, since they were resigned to spending six hours of every school day with us?

One dimension of culturally relevant teaching is the teachers' perceptions of themselves and others (see Table 3.1). Too often teachers have a poor opinion of themselves and their profession. In contrast, teachers who practice culturally relevant methods not only see themselves as professionals but also strongly identify with teaching. I begin my individual profiles of the teachers in my study with one who exemplifies this quality.

Table 3.1. Conceptions of Self and Others.

Culturally Relevant	Assimilationist
Teacher sees herself as an artist, teaching as an art.	Teacher sees herself as a technician, teaching as a technical task.
Teacher sees herself as part of the community and teaching as giving something back to the community, encourages students to do the same.	Teacher sees herself as an individual who may or may not be a part of the community; she encourages achievement as a means to escape community.
Teacher believes all students can succeed.	Teacher believes failure is inevitable for some.
Teacher helps students make connections between their community, national, and global identities.	Teacher homogenizes students into one "American" identity.
Teacher sees teaching as "pulling knowledge out"—like "mining."	Teacher sees teaching as "putting knowledge into"—like "banking."

Pauline Dupree is an African American woman who lives in the more affluent white community that borders the district where my study was carried out. She attends an African American Baptist church that many of the students and parents in the district attend. To some she appears reserved and humorless but during my two years of study, I found her to be serious and sophisticated. She describes herself as a no-nonsense, no-frills teacher.

Dupree is a slender, attractive African American woman. She is always impeccably dressed in a style that reminds one of a corporate executive. Her outfits always are coordinated; she seems to have a different pair of shoes for each. During our first interview she said that the girls in her class sometimes peek around the classroom door in the morning to see what she is wearing. When one of her students asked why she was always "so dressed up," Dupree replied that she dressed the way she did because she was coming to work and she worked with very important people, so she wanted to look good.

Dupree's classroom reflects her penchant for neatness. As the saying goes, there is a place for everything and everything in its place. Despite the fact that her class is housed in one of the school's smaller portable classrooms, she has found a way to utilize the space efficiently and avoid a sense of clutter. Stepping from the boisterous playground into her classroom is like stepping into another world. The students are well behaved and orderly—much like Pauline Dupree herself.

During our interview Dupree commented that she was somewhat dismayed at some of the young white teachers who had come to work in the district. "They come in here dressed like people going to scrub somebody's kitchen. I mean what kind of message do you send the children when you don't care enough to put on clean, pressed clothes?"

Mrs. Harris, my third-grade teacher, was quite a sharp dresser. She wore beautiful high-heeled shoes. Sometimes she switched to flats in the afternoon if her feet got tired, but every morning began with the click, click, click of her high heels as she greeted us up and down the rows. I wanted to dress the way Mrs. Harris did. I didn't want to wear old-lady comforters like Mrs. Benn's and I certainly didn't want to wear worn-out loafers like those of my first-grade teacher, Miss Schwartz. I wanted to wear beautiful, shiny, high-heeled shoes like Mrs. Harris's. That was the way a teacher should look, I thought.

Dupree's thinking about the importance of personal appearance is supported by Foster.[5] In Foster's memoirs of his years as a high school teacher in New York City, he cites several examples of students' recollections of teachers who dressed poorly. Foster suggests that in minority communities attention to personal appearance and presentation are extremely important. He describes jailed civil rights protestors who urged their lawyers to change from their blue jeans to conservative suits and to trim their long hair into more conservative haircuts so that they would look more like the prosecutor and the judge. Foster also suggests that the worst dressed teachers are white male secondary-school teachers. He believes that their feelings about the low status of teachers contribute to poor self-esteem that translates into little or no regard for how they dress.

This is clearly not the case for Pauline Dupree. She cares very much about the way she dresses. This suggests that she also cares about the people she works with and about her profession. Being a teacher is a special calling for her.

Dupree tells her fourth-grade class about teaching as a worthwhile profession.

Dupree: How many of you think you'd like to be teachers when you grow up?

(A few students raise their hands, all of them girls.)

Dupree: What about some of you boys?

(Several students snicker.)

Dupree: Don't you know how important teachers are? Without good teachers, none of the successful people you've read about would have learned the basic things like reading, writing, math, and science that helped them become successful.

Male student: But I want to make a lot of money . . . be a basketball star!

Dupree: That's a good goal, but most basketball players spend more time in classrooms than they do being basketball stars. They have short careers and they have to be prepared to do something afterward. If you're prepared educationally, you could teach. As far as money is concerned, it is true teachers don't earn as much as I think they should but there really is more to work than earning money.

Another male student: Like what, Mrs. Dupree?

Dupree: Like getting the chance to work with the most important people in the world.

Female student: Who?

Dupree: All of you. Every weekday morning when I wake up I know I'm on my way to work with the most important

people in the world. Do you know why you're the most
important people in the world?

(Silence.)

Dupree: Because you represent the future. How you turn out will
have consequences for us all. What you decide to do
with your lives can help make this community and the
world a better place. I hope a few of you will seriously
consider teaching. I'll bet quite a few of you would make
excellent teachers.

*In the midst of unpacking after one of my numerous moves, I came
across my college yearbook. In it, I spotted a photo of one of my professors. On it she had written, "Best wishes to a very capable student
who will one day go on to pursue doctoral studies." My eyes widened
in amazement; my mouth dropped open. Why on earth would she have
written that? There was nothing about me as an undergraduate that
indicated graduate school material. I didn't even know what I wanted
to do with my life back then; I'm not sure I even knew what graduate
school was or what it required.*

Teachers with Culturally Relevant Practices See Themselves as Part of the Community, See Teaching as Giving Back to the Community, and Encourage Their Students to Do the Same

This quality is very evident in Julia Devereaux's work. Devereaux
is an African American woman who has lived in the school community most of her life. She attended the very school in which
she teaches. She is active in the local Catholic church and she
serves as the local troop's Girl Scout leader. She is also the president of the district's teachers' association. None of her own three
children attended the public schools in the district. Her two
daughters went to a local black liberation school where she had
once taught (she had been married to a member of the Black
Panthers) and later went on to an exclusive white private school.

Her son currently attends a Catholic grade school that serves a largely African American and Latino population.

Devereaux's classroom is the portable one next to Dupree's. Both are fourth-grade teachers but there is a tremendous contrast in the classroom climates. Where Dupree's class is neat and orderly, Devereaux's may be described as one of "organized chaos." It is a busy classroom presided over by a busy teacher. Devereaux constantly looks for materials and supplies to purchase for her students. She takes advantage of special offers and bargains for classroom teachers offered by publishers and teacher supply stores. In consequence her room is filled to the brim with books, posters, novelty pencils, pens, erasers, key chains, coffee cups, and other interesting items. Devereaux is a scavenger who does not mind spending time looking for things that can be used in her classroom.

Along the back wall of the classroom are book shelves overflowing with books—some whole-class sets, others with random, single titles. Devereaux keeps her desk at the rear of the classroom. It has probably been some time since she has seen the top of it because it is covered with books and papers. But the condition of the desk is of little consequence to her because, as its placement in the room suggests, she spends little time there.

> This job demands that you be up and active. I don't have time to sit down at a desk. I need to be able to move in and among the children all day. I'm always saying to the kids, "Put that on my desk . . . put this on my desk." By the end of the day, so many things have been put on my desk that I can't even see it. But my teaching is not about paper, it's about people.

Devereaux believes that teaching offers a humane, ethical way for people to give back to the community. Because she is fluent in French, Devereaux could have opted to teach in a more affluent high school district. She reflects on her choice to remain in the African American community.

> I wanted to teach here so much! My first job barely paid the rent. I taught in the private black liberation school where my own kids went too. I just don't believe that you just take, take, take from the community and never give back. That's what I try to tell my students today. You've got to get a good education because the community needs your brain power.

Throughout the school day, Devereaux reminds her students of ways in which they can become more involved in the community. In addition to talking about building community, she demonstrates how to do it. She offers her home phone number to all of her students' parents. She establishes a telephone tree so that important information can get to the parents quickly.

One Friday, one of Devereaux's students did not arrive home. The student's mother called Devereaux in a panic. Devereaux reassured her that they would find the boy. She activated her telephone tree and the parents organized search parties. The student was found at the home of a friend at about 11:30 that night. Devereaux insists that she could never have done such a thing alone but because the parents worked together as a community the whole group helped in the search.

One of the persistent complaints among today's teachers is that parents are not involved enough in the schools. Teachers lament the fact that more and more children come from households where both parents work. One statistic suggests that 75 percent of parents never visit their children's schools.[6] I don't recall my parents going out of their way to come to school. Perhaps once a year they came for a conference or a student performance, but neither my mother nor my father was very visible. They were too busy working. They expected me to do what the teacher told me to do. However, if my teachers needed my parents for something, all they had to do was call.

Ann Lewis, a sixth-grade teacher, also emphasizes the idea of community. Lewis is a white woman who has lived in the community all her life. Her mother is one of the few white residents who did not participate in the "white flight" of the 1950s; she has lived in the community for more than forty years. Lewis says that it was the excellent teachers in the district she had as a child that inspired her to become a teacher. Lewis identifies strongly with the African American community; she has speech patterns similar to African American speakers. For a recent television documentary about the community and the school district, Lewis was asked by community members to be a spokesperson. She was the only white teacher that they saw as a legitimate spokesperson for the district.

Lewis and Devereaux were classmates. Now, both in their early forties, the two attended school together as girls. Like Devereaux, Lewis has been active in school district politics and preceded Devereaux as teacher association president. Indeed, she has been president of the local teachers' association at least four times.

Perhaps because of her own active community involvement, Lewis insists that her students form a viable social community before they can become a viable learning community.

> They have to care about each other and to depend on one another before we can really get anything meaningful accomplished. We have to have a sense of family, of "teamness." When we see ourselves as a team that works together, we can do anything. Having a kind of team spirit helps them to understand that one person's success is success for them all and that one person's failure is failure for everybody.

One of the ways Lewis builds community in her classroom is through her annual camping trip. Every fall semester she arranges a five-day camping trip for her students near the San Francisco Bay coastline. Organized through the county's environmental education program, Lewis and students camp out with several other groups of students. The goals are to teach about the environment, encourage cross-cultural contact, and in Lewis's case, to build a sense of togetherness and team spirit among her students.

Because many parents in the district have had negative experiences with teachers, Lewis must spend almost a month convincing some that the camping trip is a worthwhile experience and that they should grant their permission. Lewis makes sure that each student is prepared with a sleeping bag and any other necessary equipment.

Many inner-city teachers shy away from this kind of intense interaction with their students. The working hours for them are Monday through Friday, 8:30 to 3:00. Lewis's camping trip represents a sacrifice on her part, but she feels that this experience is a necessary one to mold each group of individual students into a cohesive whole.

"Well, Miss Philadelphia, when are you coming to my house for dinner?" boomed my U.S. history professor. Each of us was invited in turn as part of a group of three or four others to his home for dinner and small talk. Many years later I would be invited—actually required—to attend dinner at my graduate adviser's home. By then I understood that such gatherings served as a way to include people on the "team" and build a sense of community. My undergraduate professor was helping us understand the importance of this kind of behavior. Much of what is expected of you comes in informal learning situations. The jobs that are available, the grants being awarded, the committees most helpful for a person's advancement are issues that are not often discussed in the "neutral" classroom environment. The real business and politics of school often take place among the "community," outside of the classroom.

Teachers with Culturally Relevant Practices See Teaching as an Art and Themselves as Artists

These teachers do not ignore scientific principles of pedagogy. However, they do not view teaching as a technical skill that requires minimal training and they do not believe that as long as one follows a kind of recipe or prescription one can predict outcomes. On the contrary, teachers like Peggy Valentine exemplify the creative aspect of teaching.

Valentine,[7] an African American woman in her midforties, is relatively new to the district, having come from the Midwest after her husband's company transferred him to the West Coast. She considers herself a strict teacher and she has a flair for the dramatic, waving her arms and rolling her eyes to get a point across. She attended a historically black college and identifies closely with the students because many of them are from single-parent households and her own upbringing was in a single-parent home.

Valentine has taught in both inner-city and suburban schools. Her experiences with teaching more affluent white students has convinced her that African American students have special strengths that are rarely recognized in schools. She is very sensitive to what she perceives as slights made on the basis of race by the school administration. Her principal does not seem to like her personally but he does not hesitate to acknowledge her as one of the best teachers in the school.

Valentine enjoys teaching African American students because she says she identifies so closely with them:

> When I look at my children I see myself. I grew up in a single-parent household. I know what it is not to have the things that other children have. I also know that being smart has nothing to do with skin color. I know that some of our kids are what is called "street smart." They have what black folks call "mother wit"—you know, the kind of sense that keeps you from getting hurt or even killed. When I taught those white kids in the suburbs, of course many seemed to know "book knowledge" but more often than not some of them don't have sense enough to come in out of the rain.

Valentine creatively engages her fourth-grade students in what could otherwise be a relatively boring lesson about adjectives. To encourage the students to use more descriptive, colorful language in their writing, she has developed an activity to get them to reach for unusual adjectives. This class is held in October and so she benefits from a Halloween atmosphere. She writes a noun on the chalkboard and asks the children to think of as many words as they can to describe it. The first noun is "witch." Tentatively at first, students begin to offer some modifiers. "Old witch," says one student. "Mean witch," says another. "Black witch," offers a third. All of a sudden, Peggy grasps her chest as if she were having a heart attack and rolls her eyes back in their sockets. "Black witch, old witch, mean witch—give me a break! You guys are killin' me! I need some great, fantastic, outstanding, stupendous, magnificent adjectives. I'll even take some compound adjectives. Can anybody save me?" After a few snickers, one boy ventures, "How about a green-faced, hook-nose, evil witch?" "Yes!" shouts Peggy Valentine. "Now you're cookin' with gas. Give me more, more!" The lesson proceeds with students shouting out a variety of compound and complex adjective phrases to revive the "dying" Valentine. The lesson goes on for almost forty minutes.

In our after-lesson briefing, Valentine tells me that she had not planned the dramatic part of the lesson. However, until that point she had not felt that the students were really engaged in the lesson.

> They were just trying to get through it and I know they weren't getting anything out of it. So I decided then and there to do something dramatic to get their attention. You have to be something of an actor to be a good teacher, and sometimes you have to overact. You're on stage all of the time. I knew when I went into my "dying" act it would cause some giggles but I also know that my children *want* to please me. They want to do things right because they want my approval. In order to help them develop some motivation, I capitalize on their strong feelings for me. In my acting role, I could be angry without actually scolding them. I really planned to go about twenty-five to thirty minute on this lesson, but once they got the hang of it and seemed to really

enjoy it, I knew I couldn't cut them off. You just can't put a time limit on good teaching. You have to go with it and see where it comes out. That's why a good teacher's planning is only tentative. You can write all the behavioral objectives you want. When the dynamic of a good class gets rolling, you can't know where you're going to end up. You just have to trust that the learning has been worth it and that the kids have gotten something out of it.

Teachers with Culturally Relevant Practices Believe that All Students Can Succeed

This notion that all students can succeed may seem trite because it is constantly repeated in the pedagogical literature. However, it is not until you see it in action that you know it can be more than a slogan.

In the classrooms of assimilationist teachers—those who seem satisfied with the status quo—there is a belief that failure is inevitable for some students. Thus the teacher develops favorites, or "pets," who are often alienated from their peers. Spindler's discussion of a teacher who operates in this way is very telling about the inability of some white middle-class teachers to recognize the idiosyncratic ways in which they interact with students of different backgrounds.[8]

My fourth-grade teacher, Mrs. Powell, seemed out of place in our largely African American school. She was a middle-aged white woman who rarely smiled. I cannot remember her ever touching any of us. I do recall her saying that nobody could get an A in her class because an A would mean that we were as smart as she was. "What a bizarre notion," I thought. I worked hard to earn the A's she did not intend to give. Despite my perfect spelling, reading, and math papers she only gave me B+. My mother went to see her about the discrepancy between the papers I brought home and the grades on my report card. And from the second reporting period until the time I left her room, I received A's from Mrs. Powell. I don't think she thought I was particularly deserving of those A's, but I don't think she wanted to try to explain her unjust grading system to my mother again. Unfortunately, I don't think my mother's ability to persuade Mrs. Powell to rethink her grading extended to my classmates. My mother was able to act as my advocate but she had little impact on the overall system.

Although all of the teachers in this study demonstrated the belief that all of their students could succeed, Gertrude Winston and Elizabeth Harris will be discussed here to illustrate this quality.

Winston is a teaching veteran of forty years. She attended normal school and began teaching in a one-room school in rural Michigan. After twelve years she decided to join the Peace Corps. She had her first contact with black people as a teacher in West Africa. From West Africa she began teaching in urban schools in Southern California and eventually moved to the San Francisco Bay Area for the final years of her teaching career. She describes her experience of teaching African and African American students as transformative. She believes she has received as much from the students as she has been able to give. She is quick to share things the students have taught her about responsibility and kinship relations. She says she has never married because she has been too busy enjoying her life as a teacher.

Walk into Winston's classroom and you walk into a model of order. The room is brightly painted and there are cubicles for each student's work. All kinds of folders have been prepared to help students keep their various papers organized. Because she has her students sit at large tables rather than at desks as most of the teachers do in her school, Winston's room seems larger. Less of the floor space is taken up by individual desks. The personal touches that she has given her room are indicative of the love and care she feels for her students. She presides over a room that shouts "success." Winston insists that she has never met an unsuccessful student.

You know, they're all successful at something. The problem is that school often doesn't deal with the kinds of things that they can and will be successful at. And those tests! Those are the worst things ever. They don't begin to test what the kids really know. That's why my class is a constant search for ways to be successful. That's why we do so many projects in my class. I figure if we do enough *different* kinds of things we'll hit on the kinds of things the kids can be successful with. *Then* I look for ways to link that success with other tasks. For example, when I do my sewing bee, it's linked to my social studies unit but when a number of kids find out they're pretty good at sewing—and I mean boys as well as girls—I can get them interested in reading about sewing and other crafts and then in writing about it. But you know, the tests don't get at this big involved process of moving from a concrete experience to the level of abstraction that writing represents.

Alice Hall became my sixth-grade teacher after our original sixth-grade teacher, Mr. Moses, was promoted to assistant principal. Mr. Moses was a tall white man, one of the few male teachers at our school. While he was our teacher, he seemed to spend an inordinate amount of time chatting with Miss Plunkett, a pretty white teacher across the hall. He sat at his desk a lot. From there he told us what pages to read in our textbooks. Whenever we finished our work we were allowed to draw. I did a lot of drawing while he was our teacher.

I was one of the few students excited about Mrs. Hall's move from fourth to sixth grade. I knew her from flute club and I knew she had many talents and interests. She was a magnificent knitter and she would teach that skill to anyone who was interested. She was a gifted musician and always taught her students to play the flutophone. One of her strongest subject areas was mathematics and she helped students to delve deeply into its mysteries. Some of the students didn't like Mrs. Hall. Unlike Mr. Moses she required us to work—hard. Many students grumbled but everyone learned. Many years later I saw her at a commencement ceremony at a local college where she was a faculty member. She had become a mathematics professor.

Elizabeth Harris is a "fifty-something" African American woman who has lived in the community for more than twenty years.

She is active in a local Pentecostal congregation and is accorded the respect of a "mother of the church." Students throughout the school are careful about the kind of language they use around her. She is very gentle and soft-spoken. I describe her approach to teaching as reflective and spiritual. Her religious conviction does not permit her to see her students as failures. She sees them all as creatures of God and, accordingly, "God doesn't make junk!"

Harris, Dupree, and Devereaux all teach in the same school. Although it is situated in a white community, the residents were successful in passing an initiative that allows them to send their children to a school in a neighboring white community. Thus African American, Latino, and Pacific Islander students make the short bus ride across the freeway to attend this school. The school's principal is relatively new to the district and is not seen as effective by either her staff or the community. Harris, Dupree, and Devereaux, with their independent spirits, are not among her favorite staff members. They do not deliberately antagonize her, but neither do they kowtow to her wishes, as some of the newer faculty do.

It is not an easy school in which to teach. The school yards, halls, and a number of the classrooms seem particularly noisy. Students talk loudly and sometimes rudely to one another and to the teachers and teachers' aides. Discipline seems to be a preoccupation for many teachers.

Harris, Dupree, and Devereaux have unusual classrooms for this school; all have a sense of order and student engagement. As you walk into Harris's room you are overcome with a feeling of calm and peace. Unlike Dupree's neat and orderly, no-nonsense classroom, or Devereaux's beehive of activity, Harris's classroom seems to be an oasis in a desert or a calm place in the midst of a storm.

Harris starts her second-grade class each morning with a song. One of her children's favorites is "Peace Is Flowing Like a River." She begins instruction by asking "What are we going to be our best at today?" Students start volunteering things, both instructional and noninstructional, at which they intend to excel. "I'm gonna to be good at my math," says one little boy. "I'm gonna be good at lining up for recess," shouts another. "I'm gonna be good at doin' my own work and minding my own business," says a little girl. As the students recite their goals and expectations for the day, Mrs. Harris encourages them with a smile or a comment, "Oh, you are? Well, that's very good!" or "I just know you can do that."

At the end of the day, Harris reconvenes her students to have them assess how well they met their goals. Each student is given an opportunity to describe what she or he did to be successful during the day. Students report on successes and reflect on ways they could have been even better at some things. Harris constantly tells them how good they are.

I'm not trying to tell the children that they're something that they're not. Even though they don't all perform on grade level, we have to have a starting point for success. They need to identify for themselves what they know they can do and then do it. They also need to get credit for these accomplishments.

I see a number of our children in church. They demonstrate that they are capable of all sorts of things there. They sing in the choir, they usher, they recite, and they make announcements. I know that if they have the discipline to accomplish these adult tasks, they can certainly do the things that schools ask of them.

I think that children let too many people, like bad teachers, convince them that they are incapable of things. They give them baby work—tons and tons of silly worksheets—and never really challenge them. They need challenges. They can do it!

Teachers with Culturally Relevant Practices Help Students Make Connections Between Their Community, National, and Global Identities

This chapter began with a discussion of the ways in which some white teachers pretend not to see a child's color. But for teachers

We must see color and work to integrate culture into our lessons.

with culturally relevant practices, students' diverse cultural backgrounds are central.

Margaret Rossi is relatively new to the district. She is a former Catholic nun who has taught in another urban district and at a white suburban private school. She considers herself a "hard" teacher, and she cultivates that reputation throughout the school. She laughs at the fact that the children refer to her, behind her back, by her surname, as if they were speaking of a drill sergeant.

Rossi says she "hated" teaching at the private school because she felt the children were "neglected": they were given material things but lacked sincere parental involvement. She describes African American children as the one group of children who "will be themselves no matter what" and who will tell you exactly how they feel. "They don't try to deceive you by pretending that something is all right when deep down inside they don't think it is." Her assessment of African American children's frankness is based on experiences in both African American and white school communities. Instead of regarding these perceived differences as deficits, Rossi has called upon them as strengths.

In Rossi's class, *who* students are and how they are connected to wider communities is very important. In the class's current-events lesson, Rossi insists that the students be able to make pertinent connections between the news items they select and themselves. As the tensions increased in the Middle East prior to the Gulf War, many students brought in articles that detailed the impending conflict.

"But what does that have to do with you?" asked Rossi. "We're sitting here in sunny California, thousands of miles away from Kuwait. Why should we care?"

"Because they can drop a bomb on us!" volunteered one of her sixth graders.

"No, they can't," countered another. "We have all kinds of radar and stuff, and if they tried to fly over here, we could shoot them out of the sky."

"Let's say Rashad is right, and no planes could get through the U.S. radar," said Rossi. "What other reasons can you offer as to why these news issues would be important to us here in *this* community?"

The students sat silent for what seemed like a long time but was actually only about a minute and a half. This waiting for an answer was characteristic of Rossi's teaching style. She was not uncomfortable with classroom silence, because she believed that when you posed substantive questions with students, you were obligated to give them time to think about an answer. Finally, Denisha, a small African American girl who was a diligent student but rarely spoke up in class, raised her hand.

"Yes, Denisha?"

In a soft and measured voice, Denisha said, "Well, I think it affects us because you have to have people to fight a war, and since they don't have no draft, the people who will volunteer will be the people who don't have any jobs, and a lot of people in our community need work, so they might be the first ones to go."

Before Rossi could comment, an African American boy, Sean, chimed in. "Yeah, my dad said that's what happened in Vietnam—blacks and Mexicans were like the first ones to go."

"I'm not sure if they were the first to go," remarked Rossi, "but I can say that they were *overrepresented*." She writes these words on the board. "Do you know what I mean by this?"

None of the students volunteers a response, so Rossi proceeds with an example.

"If African Americans are 12 percent of the total U.S. population, and Latinos are 8 percent of the total U.S. population, what percent of the armed services do you think they should be?"

"Twenty percent total," calls out James, beaming at his ability to do the arithmetic quickly. "Twelve percent should be black, and 8 percent should be Mexican."

Latinx

"Okay," says Rossi. "However, I would call that 8 percent Latino rather than Mexican, because we are also including Puerto Ricans, Cuban Americans, and other U.S. citizens who are from Latin America. But in Vietnam their numbers in the armed services far exceeded their numbers in the general population. Often they were among the first to volunteer to go. Does it seem as if Denisha's comments help us link up with this news item?"

A number of the students verbally concur, while others nod in assent. As the discussion continues, students talk about the impact of having young males in particular leave their community. Given the fact that the numbers of African American and Latino males in this community are decreasing due to incarceration and other institutionalization, the prospect of losing even more men to war does not seem appealing.

By the end of the lesson, students are working in cooperative groups and creating "causality charts" where they list a number of current events and their possible impacts on their community.

In Ann Lewis's class, who students are and how they are connected to wider communities is also very important. One Monday morning, Ann writes on the board "Mandela." She asks if anyone recognizes the name. Most of the students' hands go up. South African leader Nelson Mandela has just been released after decades of political imprisonment. "I know who Mandela is," says Jerry, a sixth-grade African American boy who has strong opinions and an impressive cumulative file of school transgressions.

"Who is he, Jerry?" asks Lewis. "Well, he's this man who was in jail a long, long time in South Africa and he was fightin' for the black people's rights."

"What does Nelson Mandela have to do with us?" asks Ann. Several hands go up. Ann calls on Sugar Ray, a handsome African American boy with a trendy haircut.

"Well, like . . . Nelson Mandela represents, like, black people everywhere, not just in Africa. You know, just like Martin Luther

King was a symbol for black people not just here but all over the world."

The conversation continues as students talk about how proud they are of Nelson Mandela and how they hope his freedom will mean freedom and equality for black South Africans. Lewis suggests some books and films that students might consult to learn more about apartheid and the struggles of blacks in South Africa. Students talk animatedly about which of these they will choose to read or view. No student expresses an unwillingness to read. Even if they do not follow through with these commitments, it is clear that it is "okay" to read in this class. Reading is not seen as a "sissy" or effeminate activity.[9] The students understand both reading and film as ways to get information about things that interest them.

Teachers with Culturally Relevant Practices See Teaching as "Digging Knowledge Out" of Students

One of the commonalities among this diverse group of teachers is an overriding belief that students come to school with knowledge and that that knowledge must be explored and utilized in order for students to become achievers.

Patricia Hilliard is an African American woman in her early fifties who came to teaching after spending several years at home raising her family. After attending the local state university, she began as a long-term substitute teacher in a large urban district. She has taught in African American private schools in urban areas. She describes herself as someone who loves school and learning. Evidence of this claim is the fact that she regularly enrolls in in-service courses and workshops. She has served on statewide curriculum committees and university-funded projects on pedagogy. She sees her role in these activities as ensuring that African American children do not get short-changed when resources are allocated and policy is decided. She came to this school district as a long-term substitute but quickly demonstrated her ability to be effective with the students. The district offered her a teaching contract at the end of her substitute assignment.

Hilliard uses various methods to discover the knowledge that the students bring with them to the classroom. First, she spends time talking with parents about ways that they have educated their children. Then she talks to students about their interests and the things at which they are "experts."

> I find that much of what we claim we want to teach kids they already know in some form. I want to know what they know so that we can make some natural and relevant connections to their lives. Sometimes my black children will have information about home remedies or stories and folktales they've heard from their grandparents. We take those stories and remedies and write them up, compare notes, see how their knowledge compares with so-called traditional knowledge. I'm always amazed when students tell me things that I don't know. That happens a lot (the older I get). But it's not just about younger generation versus older generation. My students know about things like community politics and police brutality. I can't feed them a steady diet of cute little animal stories and happy middle-class kids. Their experiences have to be a part of our curriculum, too.

Hilliard's statements reflect her respect for her students' experiences. Rather than treating them as if they do not know anything, their only purpose being to come to school to learn what she wants to teach, she understands teaching as a reciprocal process. By listening and learning from the students, she understands the need to rethink and reenvision the curriculum and what she should do with it.

In sum, a focus on the children's perceptions of self and others is especially important because teachers often express feelings of low self-esteem concerning their own work.[10] These feelings are exacerbated when they work with low-income students and

children of color. The pattern for some teachers is to endure a
teaching assignment in an inner-city school until they can find
a position in a more affluent district with fewer children of color.
In contrast, several of the teachers in this study were offered
teaching positions in other districts but refused them. Their conceptions of self, students, students' parents, and community are
positive. They have made their work in the district their life's
work because they love it and are good at it. In the next chapter I
will describe how teachers' perceptions of themselves and others
affect the ways that they structure their social relations.

* 4 *

We Are Family

We was all dreamin' the same dream....
—CALVIN, A SIXTH GRADER

In Chapter Three I discussed how teachers practicing culturally relevant methods perceive themselves, their students, and
others. In this chapter I will look at how these teachers structure
social relations in their classrooms and extend those social relations into the community. I begin by looking at some of the seminal literature about the ways that classroom social relations are
structured. Next I describe some true classroom scenarios structured through assimilationist practices and suggest how culturally
relevant teaching might change them. The chapter ends with a
discussion of the ways in which culturally relevant teachers organize and structure social interactions and relations between and
among themselves and students.

Anyone who has spent time in a classroom knows that it is
among our most unusual social configurations. Scholars such as
Jackson[1] and Dreeben[2] have described extensively the routine
and regimentation of classrooms. Most of us can recall making
the transition from the typical childhood schedule of activities,
which included running, shouting, playing, asking questions, eating, and going to the bathroom whenever we felt the need, to the
seemingly bizarre routine of the classroom, where we had to sit
side by side with others yet were rarely permitted to converse.

The typical classroom is a social group where individuals
attempt to outdo one another in every academic area. Indeed,
success means doing better than others. Even in those few

instances when teachers encourage students to work in more cooperative ways, the ultimate measure of success is how well the individual does.

The role of the teacher in many classrooms is that of leader or authority figure. The teacher is regarded as all-knowing and the students as know-nothings (or at least as know-very-littles). This relationship is exacerbated in classrooms of minority students. The teacher may assume that, because of poverty, language, or culture, the students know little that is of value in a classroom setting. In these classrooms the relationships between teacher and student is hierarchical or top-down. The teacher assigns, the student carries out the assignment. The teacher talks, the student listens. The teacher asks, the student answers. Rarely are the roles reversed. Even when teachers endorse superficially more equitable classroom relations, they sometimes continue to marginalize and poorly serve students of color. However, teachers practicing culturally relevant methods understand that these typical roles can interfere with the students' ability to succeed (see Table 4.1). Consider the following two scenarios.

Table 4.1. Social Relations.

Culturally Relevant	Assimilationist
Teacher-student relationship is fluid, humanely equitable, extends to interactions beyond the classroom and into the community.	Teacher-student relationship is fixed, tends to be hierarchical and limited to formal classroom roles.
Teacher demonstrates a connectedness with all students.	Teacher demonstrates connections with individual students.
Teacher encourages a "community of learners."	Teacher encourages competitive achievement.
Teacher encourages students to learn collaboratively. Students are expected to teach each other and be responsible for each other.	Teacher encourages students to learn individually, in isolation.

Mrs. Jones and Mrs. Watson are team teachers in what is considered a progressive school program. Theirs is a classroom of first- and second-graders who participate in whole-language literacy instruction and a research-based mathematics program that capitalizes on children's thinking. There are three African American students in Jones and Watson's class, one girl and two boys. One of the boys, Lamar, is a recent transfer from a large urban district. The African American girl's mother, a university professor, volunteers once a week in the classroom. During a reading assessment she discovers that Lamar, who is of second-grade age, cannot read. The parent volunteer is routinely assigned to work with Lamar over the course of the year. Initially she attempts to interest him in the books and assignments that Jones and Watson provide. But the books are babyish; Lamar is embarrassed and reluctant to participate.

After weeks of frustration, she decides to talk more with Lamar about himself and his life before he came to this new school and community. She learns that he is an avid sports fan. Over the next weeks, she and Lamar write letters to his old friends and compose stories about his life in the city. Lamar dictates, the volunteer writes. Then Lamar reads and rereads his own constructions. Together they devise a kind of "concentration" game, using the names of sports teams and the cities in which they are located. Each week Lamar seems to look forward to the forty-five minute session he spends with the volunteer.

By the end of the year, Lamar is beginning to read. Almost all of his reading instruction has come as a result of the sessions with the volunteer. Two months before the end of the school year, the volunteer is asked to include the other African American boy, Marcus, in the weekly sessions. To her dismay, she learns then that Marcus hadn't been able to read either. Her own daughter was reading before she entered the class; she has complained to her mother that the teachers "don't teach me anything."

Mrs. Cook has been teaching kindergarten for almost thirty years. She describes her approach as eclectic. She believes in paying close attention to the developmental needs of the students. The five-year-olds in her class have the opportunity to make lots of choices. Much of their work is organized around activity centers. Each morning the students convene on the rug to participate in the morning routine that includes roll call, calendar activity, and sharing. Then Cook divides them into activity groups and dismisses them to activity centers. Matthew, the only African American boy in the class, rushes to his activity table and completes the activity within a few minutes. Impatient to move on to the next table, he complains to the students there that they are taking too long. Cook reprimands Matthew for his tone with the other children. Matthew begins to wander around the room looking for something to do. Cook tells him to take his seat. Back at his original table Matthew teases one of the students about being so slow. Cook tells Matthew that he is not being kind and must go to the "time-out corner." Matthew slowly and angrily makes his way to the lonely chair. Cook looks at Matthew with a grim face. "We go through this every day," she thinks to herself. Later in the morning, on the playground at recess, several of the students chant, "Bad boy, bad boy, Matthew is a bad boy." Matthew angrily strikes out at one of the chanters and the teacher on duty sends him to the principal's office for hitting another child.

Both of these real-life scenarios offer examples of assimilationist teaching practices. In neither one is the teacher intentionally bad or malicious. However, by failing to incorporate the African American students into the community of learners, these teachers foster the alienation that these African American students are likely to experience increasingly as their school careers progress.

In the first example, Jones and Watson have ignored the educational needs of the African American children. Unsure of what to say or do with them, the teachers leave them alone. The African American girl is able to negotiate the class by herself, but the first boy is totally dependent on the volunteer for instruction, and the second is ignored until the teachers realize that their laissez-faire strategy has not helped him to learn to read.

In the second example, Cook turns Matthew's strengths into weaknesses. Clearly ahead of the other students in his class, Matthew races through his activities, which fail to provide him with an intellectual challenge. Instead of offering additional intellectual stimulation for him, Cook punishes him when he attempts to seek his own stimulation. As this becomes a daily ritual—Matthew's finishing his work at the activity center first, then bothering other children, then wandering around the room, and finally being sent to the time-out corner—the other students begin to view Matthew as outside of the classroom community. Thus in kindergarten he already has the reputation of a "bad boy." Unless someone or something intervenes, this perception of Matthew is likely to follow him throughout his school career and become a self-fulfilling prophecy.

I will try to demonstrate in the next section how culturally relevant teaching helps students work collectively toward a common goal of academic and cultural excellence. The ways in which the social structure and classroom culture is managed affects their willingness to work toward a common goal. How might culturally relevant teaching have handled the situations in the described scenarios?

In the first situation, such a teacher would have sought to help all of the students develop high skills because the failure of one to meet high standards would reflect upon the entire group. Students might have been challenged to come up with strategies to ensure that all of their classmates met the expectations. Instead of shifting the responsibility for teaching Lamar to a volunteer, such a teacher might have used the volunteer to work with more successful students while she herself worked more intensively with Lamar.

Recognizing that both Lamar and Marcus were failing to thrive in the class, such a teacher might have developed different strategies for intensifying instruction for the boys: perhaps a regular schedule of individualized instruction, or a conference with the boys' parents about how all might work together to improve their reading skills, or more flexible scheduling of a series of reading volunteers to ensure that the boys received more regular instruction.

In the second situation, culturally relevant teaching would have recognized Matthew's intellect as a positive that could be used to help other students. Given the role of monitor or partner to slower students, he could have become the resource person who helped everyone complete assigned activities more quickly. Instead of being known as a "bad boy," Matthew might have become the very student that the others wanted to have assist them. In this way, Matthew would have developed a deeper understanding of the concepts and skills that Cook was attempting to teach and reinforce.

We're All in This Together

In his seminal study, Rist revealed that tracking of students occurs almost as soon as they enter school and that the criteria by which they are tracked often is arbitrary.[3] Students who fail to look, talk, or act as the teacher does are in danger of being placed in the lowest tracks.[4] Placement in these low tracks is likely to mean less attention and individualized instruction from the teacher. In a kind of self-fulfilling prophecy, these students, who have had little instruction, perform at lower levels. Their ability to rise above these levels is compromised because they have had less attention. Thus they continue a cycle of poor school performance that was initiated by a teacher's biases and predispositions toward them.

Because of a clerical error I ended up in a "basic" English class during the first grading period of my sophomore year. Unaware of the way that students were tracked in the school, I was excited about the opportunity to be in a class where African American students were the majority.

In my previous English classes the emphasis was on literature and composition. We read Dickens, Hardy, and Shakespeare. But in this class we were drilled in grammar and spelling. Each week we took a spelling test. Each week I got 100. In fact, I got an A on every assignment given. Nevertheless, on the first report card my grade was a C. When I questioned the teacher about it, she smiled and said, "Why Gloria, a C is the highest grade possible in this class!"

After a quick trip to my guidance counselor, the placement error was detected. I was returned to my rightful place in the college preparatory English class. The basic English teacher told me she was sorry to see me go and wished me well. I left that class confused and hurt. Why hadn't the teacher recognized that I had the ability to move out of it? And more importantly why didn't my classmates know that no matter how hard they worked, their efforts would only be rewarded with mediocre grades?

Cooperative learning has become a popular response to ability-group tracking.[5] It is premised on the notion that students can and should learn together and from one another. The techniques associated with cooperative learning are being implemented in many classrooms. Each of the teachers who participated in my study uses some form of cooperative learning techniques in their teaching. However, the underlying ideology that informs their use of these strategies is to prepare their students for collective growth and liberation. Rather than elevate the importance of individual achievement, the teachers encourage their students to work within a collective structure and reward group efforts more often than individual ones. Even in discussions of heroes or role models, several of the teachers expose the underlying group structure and support that boosted the individuals to excellence.

For example, rather than allow her students to rely on the traditional romantic story of the individual Rosa Parks—the seamstress-turned-civil-rights-activist—Dupree provides her students with a more accurate picture:

Now I know your book talks about Rosa Parks being a seamstress with tired feet who decided to sit down on a bus one day. But, that's not the *whole* story. . . . You see, Rosa was an activist. (She writes the word "activist" on the chalkboard.) That means she was someone who didn't wait for things to happen. She made things happen! For years Rosa had been going to a place called Highlander Folk School (she writes "Highlander Folk School" on the board) learning how to educate black people in their struggle against racism. She was a member of the local NAACP and was just waiting for a chance to confront racism. She was a woman with a plan.

This story teaches us that we can't just do something without thinking first. You can't do things you're not prepared to do. And you probably can't do very much all by yourself. You need help. I need help. We all need help. That's how we make things happen—by working together.

The Teacher-Student Relationship in the Culturally Relevant Classroom Is Fluid and "Humanely Equitable"

In Peggy Valentine's class this kind of relationship[6] sometimes means that she takes a seat at a student desk and prods one of her African American students up to the front to be the teacher. "All right, you're the teacher," she calls. "Explain to me what you mean. Teach me how to do it." The student begins to explain a process or a concept to Valentine. Throughout the explanation Valentine waves her hand in the air, asking the student-turned-teacher to slow down or go over something again. Sometimes she takes notes frantically. At other times she gazes at the student with a puzzled look. With the skill of an experienced teacher, the student probes Valentine by asking whether she understands. The range and variety of areas in which Valentine asks her students to provide leadership is wide; sometimes she asks about mathematics or language, at others she requests details about student culture, for example, what the words of a popular song are or what they mean. The students are used to seeing her in the role of student and themselves in the role of teacher and they seem comfortable with this role reversal.

Patricia Hilliard defines her relationship with the students as that of an extended family. Each school year begins with the shaping of an "undefined contract." She is flexible about specific classroom expectations and helps the students formulate expectations they can meet and consequences they can live with. Further, the students form "extended family groups" within the classroom and even make up names for the families. The only prohibitions Hilliard places on the names are that they cannot be offensive or have gang connotations. In their groups, students are responsible for monitoring one another's academic work and personal behavior and for solving group problems. Family members may talk with one another and provide academic assistance. Although testing is individual, test results reflect on the whole family. A Hilliard discussion goes like this:

Hilliard: What happens in your house when you do something good?
Student: My momma is real happy.
Hilliard: How do you know she's happy?
Student: Sometimes she hugs and kisses me. Sometimes she just smiles and tells me.
Hilliard: Right! And that's what we're going to do here. When your "family member" does a good job you're going to show him or her just how proud you are. And when someone doesn't do a good job, you're not going to laugh at him or tease him. You're going to do your best to help him do better. When one of us does well, we all do well. When one of us fails, we all fail.

Culturally Relevant Teaching Involves Cultivation of the Relationship Beyond the Boundaries of the Classroom

My parents rarely came to school. With the exception of a special student production or parent-teacher conference that took place in the evenings, they didn't come to school. "Your job is to do well in school," my mother insisted. I never received money or incentives for good grades. Good grades were expected. However, more important than grades was deportment. "Even if you're dumb you can sit still and behave yourself," my mother said. Teacher notes or calls about behavior were not tolerated.

In my home, the schoolhouse door was a threshold for children, a boundary for parents. But my parents did have access to my teachers. De facto racial segregation meant that several of my teachers lived in or near my neighborhood. They attended our church. They shopped in neighborhood stores. They patronized local barbers and beauticians. Opportunities to interact with my parents and keep them appraised of my school performance were numerous. My teachers knew me as a student and as a person.

Because many African American students live in and attend schools in communities that their teachers neither live in nor choose to frequent after school hours means that few have the opportunity to interact with their teachers outside the classroom. Teachers who practice culturally relevant methods work to find ways to facilitate this out-of-school (or at least out-of-the-classroom) interaction.

Elizabeth Harris cultivates relationships with her students that extend beyond the classroom doors. As an active member of her local church, she relies heavily on her commitment to her faith to assist her pedagogically:

> You've got to realize that being with the children for five or six hours a day is just not enough for the kind of impact you want to have on them. The stuff they're exposed to on TV and in the movies, the music, the streets…all of this is vying for their hearts and minds. They need a chance to see things and live their lives in ways that nurture them. I know that I'm not here to try to convert them, religiously I mean, but I do feel an obligation to give them a glimpse of their spiritual side.

In order to provide that spiritual glimpse Harris asks students who are interested in attending Sunday school to have their parents telephone her at home. This semester, two parents follow up and call. Harris arranges to pick the children up on Sunday morning. She takes her two charges to a local fast food restaurant for breakfast and then off to Sunday school. As their Sunday school teacher, Harris not only imparts the tenets of her faith but also works with the students on reading, writing, and speaking. By Monday morning word has spread about the free breakfast, and several other students ask if they can go next time. Harris reminds them that their parents must call first. Within three weeks, eight or nine students are regularly attending Harris's Sunday school class. She now arranges for the students to meet in front of the public school and she and her husband pick them up. The fast food breakfast gives way to a special treat like muffins or doughnuts at Sunday school. By the end of the year, almost half of her students have attended the Sunday school class at least once. Several students no longer meet at the school but go to the Sunday school class directly, taking one or more of their siblings with them.

Harris talks candidly about balancing her roles as a state-employed public school teacher and dedicated church worker:

> I know that I have to be careful about this religious thing. I offer it as a suggestion to the children just one time. I don't hound them about it. I don't penalize anybody for not going and I don't give special privileges in the classroom to those who do. You know, most of these children have been to church before but we're living in times when parents are so tired by the end of the week that Sunday school is the furthest thing from their minds. I just want to do whatever I can to get to know the children better. The Sunday school classroom gives me a chance to work with them without the pressure of grades and tests. You know, they're learning all the time.

Julia Devereaux, active in her church, uses other organizations to interact with her students outside of the classroom. A long-time

Girl Scout leader, Devereaux actively recruits the girls in her class into her troop.

> I just bring all of the membership information here and tell the girls how wonderful scouting can be. Frankly, by the time I describe the sleepovers—overnight camping—and the skating party, everyone says they want to be in the troop. They don't all follow up but enough of them do that I seem to see my school kids almost everyday! (She laughs.)

In addition to the Girl Scouts, Devereaux regularly invites students to her home for dinner or Saturday lunch. They interact with her own children, particularly her high-school-age daughter and eight-year-old son. (Her oldest daughter no longer lives at home.) Known for her healthy appetite, she plans classroom activities that include meals. When her students study about customs and traditions celebrated by African Americans, Devereaux helps them plan a soul-food dinner. As they enjoy the various dishes, students are asked to learn about the significance of the foods. Her students speak authoritatively about yams, okra, and black-eyed peas as West African staples. They talk about why pork became so prevalent in African American diets and the health hazards associated with eating high-fat, high-sodium foods. Several students present research on the incidence of high blood pressure and strokes among African Americans. Devereaux sees these "food festivals" as an integrated way to teach a variety of things:

> The students are always being blamed for things they don't know. I mean, people will complain that the kids are wild in the cafeteria, but how many chances do they have at school to sit down, eat a decent meal presented in an appealing way, and have a civil conversation? When we have our little food activities I try to make them really nice. We have place mats, napkins,

the whole bit. You'd think we were sitting in a fancy, downtown restaurant. (She laughs.)

Patricia Hilliard also structures some of her social relationships with her students around food and eating. Once a week, she selects a group of four or five of them to join her for lunch. The students, almost all of whom participate in the school's free lunch program, are given a note to take to the cafeteria that allows them to get their lunches and bring them back to the classroom. When they return with their lunches, they find that Hilliard has prepared a table with place mats and napkins. The students sit and chat with Hilliard as they eat lunch. The thirty to forty minutes are spent talking about the students' and Hilliard's lives and interests. There is almost no talk about school or school work. They become a group of friends having lunch together.

> I think I use the "lunch bunch" thing for a lot of reasons. First off, it's a way to get to know the students. The pace of the classroom is so frantic that you hardly have time to get to know them as people. I also use it to help me with discipline. You know, I think the thing that causes discipline problems is that we just don't know the kids well enough. We don't know what makes them tick...what they like, what they don't like . . . and they don't know each other very well. I think that's what contributes to their fighting each other.

It is interesting to note that these lunchtime gatherings may be in violation of the state education code, which says something to the effect that students are required to have at least thirty minutes of lunchtime away from their teachers. It also may violate the teachers' union contract, which insists that teachers have a forty-five-minute duty-free lunch. Both Devereaux and Hilliard comment that they have "conveniently ignored" those rules and guidelines that interfere with their ability to know their students better.

Teachers with Culturally Relevant Practices Are Careful to Demonstrate a Connectedness with Each of Their Students

Instead of idiosyncratic and individualistic connections with certain students, these teachers work to assure each student of his or her individual importance.[7] Although it has been suggested that teachers unconsciously favor those students perceived to be most like themselves (or some ideal) in race, class, and values, culturally relevant teaching means consciously working to develop commonalities with all the students.[8]

Margaret Rossi recognizes that because she is white, female, and a former nun, she may seem to have little or nothing in common with her class of African American students, most of whom are lower income and few of whom are Catholic. However, Rossi has developed a technique to draw the students out, to share their interests, and to introduce them to new interests. She begins each school year by giving each student an "entry questionnaire." In addition to gathering up-to-date and important information about their addresses, phone numbers, and birthdays, Rossi discovers what students do outside of school, how they spend their leisure time, and which subjects they like and which they do not.

> I try to find out as much as I can about the students early in the school year so I can plan an instructional program that motivates them and meets their needs. You'd be surprised how many kids tell me that nobody has ever bothered to even ask them what they like. The entry questionnaire is also a great way to learn a little about their reading and writing levels. I think that it's hard for sixth graders in a community like this one to trust, white people especially. They've been lied to too many times. I don't blame them for not wanting to open up with me right away. But soon enough they begin to see that I take the information they give me to heart.

Taking the students' information "to heart" means that Rossi acknowledges each student's birthday with a personal card.

Without much fanfare she places a birthday card on the student's desk that morning and announces the birthday to the class. Students in middle-class schools have similar experiences from their early grades on. By sixth grade, this kind of birthday ritual may hold little or no significance for them. However, Rossi's acknowledgment usually brings a smile and a thank you from her preadolescent students. Such personal acknowledgments support the students' sense of self—they are seen as "real people" by their teacher.

These small acts of kindness and civility seem ordinary to those who have come to expect them as a fact of life. However, for many inner-city children this is not the case. In a recent visit to a large midwestern city, I visited an eighth-grade social-studies class in an inner-city middle school. The school's population was 85 to 90 percent African American.

I asked the students to explain their class curriculum to me. They quickly recited a litany of typical eighth-grade social-studies topics. "Oh, you know," one young girl began, "the Constitution: the preamble and the amendments, the Articles of Confederation, stuff like that."

I remarked that the things she mentioned did not sound particularly exciting, yet the students seemed to like the class. "What is it that you like about the class?

"The teacher!" they responded in unison.

"What do you like about the teacher?" I probed.

"She listens to us!"

"She respects us!"

"She lets us express our opinions!"

"She looks us in the eye when she talks to us!"

"She smiles at us!"

"She speaks to us when she sees us in the hall or in the cafeteria!"

Their responses seemed so ordinary. They were describing simple acts of human kindness, yet it was apparent that much of their school experiences had been devoid of such kindnesses. As I reflected on the culturally relevant teaching I had been observing for three years I felt comforted by the fact that I could document this kind of reaffirmation of the students' humanity in all of the classes I observed. Even when students were reprimanded, their dignity and basic humanity were not attacked. Like the Asian notion of personal (and familial) honor, the teachers always found a way to make sure the students did not "lose face."

Another way that Margaret Rossi incorporates students' interests into the classroom is by decorating the walls with posters of their favorite sports heroes and film stars. The posters serve as prompts for their writing. Rossi encourages the students to write letters to and essays about these celebrities. As the students grow accustomed to writing such pieces, Rossi helps them use their writing skills to craft editorial letters to newspapers. Moving in this way from the students' interests and community culture to broader uses for these interests helps Rossi improve their academic achievement.

Teachers with Culturally Relevant Practices Encourage a Community of Learners

Encouraging a community of learners[9] means helping the students work against the norm of competitive individualism.[10] The teachers believe that the students have to care, not only about their own achievement but also about their classmates' achievement.

As already mentioned, Patricia Hilliard makes her classroom into an "extended family":

> I use the family metaphor because I really believe it. When children are mean and disrespectful to one another, I remind them that they're showing that disrespect to one of their brothers or sisters. You have to drill that notion in them over and over. It sounds like overkill but it's the way I teach them to get along.

I have to remind myself too that we're family. I mean, I sometimes ask myself, "What would I do if this child were one of my own?" That's a pretty good measure of how I ought to treat my students.

Hilliard and other teachers' notions about building an extended family are consistent with some of the psychological literature that refutes the notion of poor self-concept among African American students. This view suggests that African American connections to African cultural norms support a very different view of self: "Some non-Western world views, particularly the African, place a totally different emphasis on self, conceiving of the self as coming into being as a consequence of the group's being. . . . The African world view suggests that 'I am because we are and because we are, I am.' In so emphasizing, this view makes no real distinction between the self and others. They are in a sense one and the same. . . . One's self-identity is therefore always a people identity, or what could be called an . . . extended self."[11]

Ann Lewis takes the building of a community of learners to another level. As mentioned in Chapter Three, Lewis plans a beginning-of-the-school-year camping trip in order to solidify the sense of cooperation and interdependence she feels is crucial for the kind of classroom she believes works best for her students. She believes that this "sense of teamness" that the students cultivate during the camping trip carries over into the classroom.

Lewis's camping trip is a part of a larger environmental education program sponsored by the county office of education. Originally designed to teach environmental education and to promote desegregation (students from schools throughout the county use the camp), the camping trip provides Lewis with an opportunity to teach her students some important cooperative skills:

Not many people relish the idea of being in the woods with twenty-seven kids for a week. I'm not so sure I really relish the idea myself. But it is so important to help the kids see that we're all in this together. It's not as if they don't know about teamwork. They play on sports teams and sing together in church choirs, that kind of stuff. But, you know, they don't think of their classroom as a place where they can be team members.

Culturally Relevant Teaching Encourages Students to Learn Collaboratively and Expects Them to Teach Each Other and Take Responsibility for Each Other

Despite the plethora of programs and activities that have adopted aspects of cooperative learning as instructional strategies, very little real cooperation is taught or required in the classroom.[12] Students may have opportunities for group work, but what teachers deem cooperative behavior more accurately falls under the category of compliance or conformity. Culturally relevant teaching advocates the kind of cooperation that leads students to believe they cannot be successful without getting help from others or without being helpful to others.

Gertrude Winston thinks that the cooperative nature of her classroom is compatible with her students' home culture:

I have the feeling that there is not a lot of competition among siblings at home, so in the classroom we do a lot of sharing. Everybody helps everybody else to succeed. The students are always willing to help somebody else learn something.

Further, Winston says that she learned an important lesson about the cooperative spirit when she began teaching African American children:

I notice a great deal of caring that black youngsters give to siblings. I mean, when I share something they always save part of it to take home to share.

Winston regularly gives two parties in her class, one at Halloween and one at Christmas. This semester, students volunteer to bring in treats to share with their classmates at Halloween. Winston purchases and brings in all of the treats for the Christmas party. At her first Christmas party with African American students, Winston bought what she felt were more than enough treats for the class. But no sooner than she had passed out the goodies than several students began to ask for more. When she inquired as to what they had done with the treats she had distributed, the students indicated that they had wrapped them up to take home to a family member. They were now asking for something for themselves.

> From that day on I knew to buy twice as many candies and treats for the children. No matter what we have or how much I try to tell them differently, they make sure that that first portion goes to that brother or sister or baby cousin. I think that's kind of nice. It is what caring and cooperation are all about, putting someone else's wants and needs before your own.

For Pauline Dupree, student cooperation and mutual responsibility are necessities. Dupree's classroom is rigorous and demanding. Students do lots of reading and writing every day. The assignments and activities seem nonstop. By design, there is no way to complete all that she gives them to do without cooperation. Thus Pauline requires that each student have a "study buddy."

> From the day that they walk into my room they know they have to select a buddy. This is their learning partner for the year. A lot of times when a student is having a hard time I'll call the buddy to my desk and really give him or her an earful. "Why are you letting your buddy struggle like this? What kind of partner are you? You're supposed to be the helper." Within a couple of months I begin to see them looking out for one another. One student will hesitate

before he turns in his paper and will go check to make sure the buddy is doing okay. Eventually, they begin to check very carefully and they may discover some errors that they themselves have made. Having the buddy is really just another level of learning. Those that are helping are really helping themselves.

One of the concerns that teachers voice about fostering such cooperative structures in the classroom involves how to evaluate individuals when the focus is on the group. None of the teachers in this study see this as a problem. They indicate that teachers have a wealth of information about students' abilities and achievement levels. Indeed, they voice concern about an overreliance on standardized tests as a true measure of student achievement. Gertrude Winston comments:

I don't think anybody ever truly measures what the children know. They give tests that have nothing to do with what we're trying to do. They never give a test that measures the children's ability to think through difficult problems, to come up with a variety of solutions. Some of our children have a lot of wisdom. They've seen a lot of things, been through a lot. You have to be smart to weather the kinds of storms some of these kids have been through. But you know they're not going to make a test that measures that kind of stuff.

The kind of teaching advocated by these teachers seeks to help students see community-building as a lifelong practice that extends beyond the classroom. Living in a community ravaged by drugs, unemployment, underemployment, high drop-out rates, high crime, and poverty spawns an innate pessimism in the children. They fail to see how they can succeed unless it is at the expense of others. Thus the teachers have to work hard to help them see beyond the decimation caused by federal, state, and county neglect to the real strengths of their community.

In Ann Lewis's class, a student remarked, "I hate this community. I can't wait till I grow up and move away from it." Lewis calmly asked, "Do you hate your parents? Do you hate the church you attend? Do you hate the friends you play with each day? Do you hate me?" To each of these questions the student replied no. Lewis explained to him (and, of course, to the rest of the class) that all of these things she mentioned made up the *real* community. The drugs and the crime had invaded the community and if the students did not learn how to build it up, they would overrun it. Rather than suggest to the students that their education should take them away from their community, Lewis was reinforcing the idea that it would give them the power to make their community what they wanted it to be.

Psychological safety is a hallmark of each of these classrooms. The students feel comfortable and supported. They realize that the biggest infraction they can commit is to work against the unity and cohesiveness of the group. However, that sense of solidarity or "teamness" cannot be used as an excuse for individuals to follow the group mindlessly. The teachers regularly challenge individuals to confront group thinking to ensure that the highest standards—intellectual, cultural, and ethical—are maintained.

Mrs. Valentine uses activities from a curriculum innovation of the 1970s known as *values clarification*, which was based on the premise that all students come to school with values, and that it is the teacher's role to help the students understand or clarify these values. Rather than attempt to shape or indoctrinate the students with a particular set of values, the curriculum serves to help students examine what they believe and why they believe it.[13] During one observation, Valentine told the story of the Alligator River. The story is about a moral dilemma. To resume briefly, a girl named Abigail attempts to win the affections of a boy named Gregory. In an effort to prove her love and loyalty, Abigail promises to get Gregory's eyeglasses repaired across the Alligator River. Because the bridge has been washed out, Abigail prevails on a boy named Sinbad to ferry her across. Sinbad agrees on the condition that Abigail steal a radio for him.

Abigail asks another friend, Ivan, to help her make her decision. Not wanting to get involved, Ivan tells Abigail he cannot help. So Abigail agrees to Sinbad's terms. After she steals the radio, Sinbad ferries her across the river and she gets Gregory's eyeglasses repaired.

When Abigail returns and tells Gregory of the trouble she has gone through for him, he is repulsed. He tells her he cannot date a girl who is a thief. Distraught, Abigail seeks comfort from another friend, Slug, who promptly confronts Gregory and beats him up. The story ends with Abigail laughing at the battered Gregory.

Valentine asked each student to rank the story's characters from the most to the least reprehensible. When all the students finished with their rankings they had to join into teams, which then had to come up with team rankings. In their teams, the students had to make convincing arguments for their personal rankings in an attempt to sway their group's members.

Valentine's students engaged in lively discussion about their views. They presented reasoned arguments with real-life examples to illustrate their points.

Girl: Well, I think Abigail was the worst because she just didn't know how to think for herself. I mean, if she just used her own brain she would know that stealing that radio was stupid. She didn't even think about what would've happened if she got caught.

Boy: But Sinbad was the real bad one because he's the one that came up with the whole bad idea. He was takin' advantage of her cause he knew how bad she wanted a ride. I know people who try to do that. I mean they be sayin' stuff like, "Yeah, I'll help you out man but you gotta do my homework, or wash my dishes," or stuff like that.

Girl: I'm not saying that Sinbad wasn't bad, but Abigail is really
        the baddest one. Look, if she just said, "Hey, I'm not even
        going to be stealing no radio for nobody," then the whole
        thing would've been over. You have to be able to stand
        up to people when they put stupid stuff up in your face.
        If I was Abigail I'd say, "How you gonna play me? I just
        asked you for a ride. If you can't do it just say no. Don't
        be trying to get me in trouble." I think Sinbad would
        have respected her more if she just stood up to him. The
        same thing happens every day. People be trying to get
        you to do stuff that you know is wrong—like asking you
        to stand on a corner and look out for the police while
        they selling "hubbas" [crack cocaine]. Now you know
        it's wrong and you have to be able to say "No, I'm not
        even getting into that." 'Cause if you don't they gonna
        keep coming back to you because they know you're weak
        and the next thing you know you sitting up at Hillcrest
        [juvenile detention center].

Although these value clarification activities were originally
designed to help students understand their own values, Valentine
feels that they are more useful in helping students make decisions
about when to go along with the group and when to challenge it.
According to Valentine,

Decision making is one of the most important skills the kids can
develop. They are confronting so many competing interests out
there. They have to learn how to work together in the classroom
and have a sense of solidarity so that we can accomplish some
things, but they can't have a herd mentality that allows them to
just go along with anything the group says. I don't just do this as a
feel-good activity. We develop a lot of speaking and writing skills
as we go through these activities. I have the students write out
their positions on the various issues. I sometimes set up debates

around the values and role-playing activities. My kids have had so many experiences that are devalued in the classroom. They are often in critical situations without the skills to make decisions in their own best interests. The classroom has got to be the kind of place that helps them deal with their lives *now* so they can have some options, some choices, later.

Concluding Thoughts

In sum, culturally relevant teaching fosters the kinds of social interactions in the classroom that support the individual in the group context. Students feel a part of a collective effort designed to encourage academic and cultural excellence. As members of an extended family, the students assist, support, and encourage one another. The entire group rises and falls together. Thus it is in everyone's best interest to ensure that the others in the group are successful.

There is little reward for individual achievement at the expense of others. Even when individuals achieve on their own—inside or outside of the classroom—the teachers frame that achievement in a group context. They say things like, "Look what that member of our class did. Aren't *we* proud of that? Don't we have some brilliant people in our family?"

By supporting the academic community, teachers encourage the sense of belonging that young people crave. The "school gang" becomes a viable alternative to the street gang.

Culturally relevant teaching honors the students' sense of humanity and dignity. Their complete personhood is never doubted. Self-worth and self-concept is promoted in a very basic way, by acknowledging the individual's worthiness to be a part of a supportive and loving group.

My own teachers encouraged me and demanded nothing less than excellence. They made me feel smart and I responded. But there was still something wrong with my education. There were lots of smart kids in my elementary school, but they weren't all as economically stable as I was—I came from a working-class family with a father who was a laborer and a mother who was a clerk. I remember one girl in particular; her name was Portia. She was the smartest person I had ever met. She could sum a column of numbers with lightning speed. She could reason beyond her years. But she almost never came to school with her hair combed. Her teeth had not seen a toothbrush in years and she often smelled of urine. I liked her because she was smart and had a great sense of humor. It did not bother me that her house was dark, smelled funny, and had furniture that looked like the kind of stuff people set out curbside to be collected with the trash. I lost track of Portia after elementary school. She did not attend the junior high school I went to across town. The last time I saw her was in eleventh grade. Portia was pregnant and had dropped out of school. As smart as I believed I was, I knew I was not as smart as Portia. So why wasn't she on the fast track to college? Why had she been passed over in the academic shuffle?

In the next chapter I will examine how culturally relevant teaching helps students understand, confront, and create knowledge. Rather than being viewed unproblematically, the school curriculum becomes something that both students and teachers struggle with to create knowledge. For example, the social studies curriculum might suggest that labor unions worked to defend the rights of workers. However, students and teachers may come from homes where parents and grandparents were barred from the same unions. Instead of passively dismissing either the curriculum version or the real-life experiences of students and/or teachers, teachers feel a responsibility to help students grapple with the contradictions.

Fully aware that curriculum panels and school boards often are charged with deciding on a symbolic curriculum designed to satisfy community or interest-group demands (banning sex education when students are immersed in a sex-saturated society, for example), culturally relevant teaching involves students in the knowledge-construction process, so that they can ask significant questions about the nature of the curriculum. The ultimate goal is to ensure that they have a sense of ownership of their knowledge—a sense that it is empowering and liberating. As coconstructors in the knowledge-building process, they are less alienated from it and begin to understand that learning is an important cultural activity.

* 5 *

The Tree of Knowledge

dream: n. 1. a sequence of sensations, images, thoughts, etc., passing through a sleeping person's mind 2. a fanciful vision of the conscious mind; daydream; fantasy; reverie 3. a fond hope or aspiration.

Almost every prospective teacher is aware of a taxonomy of learning that situates "knowledge" at the first level of cognition. Although it is the building block that other levels of cognition rest upon, it represents a basic level of thinking. In general, knowledge is understood to encompass basic recall and recognition of facts. Yet it is about this basic level of learning that much educational debate occurs.

Scholars and teachers alike are coming to see knowledge as a social construction. In 1970 Kuhn broke new ground in mainstream scholarship when he described the ways in which all scientists (social, behavioral, and natural) create knowledge and use implicit cultural assumptions, perspectives, and frames of reference in doing so.[1] Nowhere are these implicit assumptions, perspectives, and frames of references of greater concern than in the school curriculum.

Although I got better grades in math and science, social studies was my favorite subject in high school. Insecure and lacking confidence in math and science, I studied them religiously. I took every word of the teacher and the text as gospel. I memorized classification systems in biology, periodic tables in chemistry, theorems and postulates in geometry, and formulas in algebra. At test time, I dutifully repeated (indeed, regurgitated) exactly what was in my notes and the textbook.

For me, math and science were about "right answers." But social studies was a different animal altogether.

Despite only a grade school education, my father had an informed opinion about things historical, economic, and political. He quizzed both my brother and me about items in the newspaper and on television newscasts. The changing world of the late 1950s and the early 1960s was a gold mine for my father's inquisitive prodding. I read all I could to enter into debate with him on all kinds of social issues.

The social studies classroom was a place to display my intellect. It was the place where I came alive. For my final project in U.S. history, I did a term paper on the African slave trade. With the help of a scholar in African American history and a trip to the renowned Schomburg Library collection in New York, I wrote what I believed to be a well-documented, insightful paper. My teacher never returned the paper, claiming he had misplaced it. He insisted that it deserved a B. I never got a chance to see his written comments, but I knew in my heart that it had been an A paper.

In recent years there has been debate about conflicts between what has been regarded as the literary canon and what is historical fact. We now ask if the canon represents a culturally specific set of understandings or objective truths. For example, was the ancient Egyptian civilization black? And did Columbus discover, or conquer, or contact? These kinds of questions should present exciting challenges and learning opportunities. Instead, they have led to vitriolic debates and accusations from all sides about both our educational system and western civilization.[2]

At the university level, conservatives have railed against the notion that African American writers like Alice Walker are taught more often than Shakespeare (a claim empirically disproved by Graff).[3] Two widely read and quoted books, Bloom's *The Closing of the American Mind*[4] and Hirsch's *Cultural Literacy*,[5] have led the call for a return to a Western civilization tradition that would save "us" from the "barbarians at the gate."

For advocates of multiculturalism the questions are "Us" refers to whom? And "barbarians" refers to whom? At the precollege level, states including New York and California have struggled with the tension between unity and diversity in developing social studies curricula.[6] In California, the unity view has won out, corrupting the democratic process through which curriculum and textbook adoption takes place.[7] In New York, the diversity view has won, no thanks to stinging criticism from noted historians like Kenneth Jackson and Arthur Schlesinger, Jr. Scholars and community members who had argued for the promotion of diverse perspectives were labeled "extremists" and "demagogues."

Amid all this argument, parents and teachers are left with the task of selecting and implementing curricula for students who ultimately must be prepared to survive and thrive in a democratic and multicultural society. Aware of the potential impact that parents of grade school students could have on school curriculum and policy, Hirsch began translating his notions of a "core curriculum" into popular books for parents such as *What Your First Grader Needs to Know* (1991) and *What Your Second Grader Needs to Know* (1991).

However, in most low-income communities and communities of color it is neither the national commissions, the state boards, nor the local districts that affect the education of the students, it is the teachers. Whether they exercise it or not, classroom teachers (particularly in these communities) have great power in determining the official curriculum.

Apple points out that much of the discourse about curriculum has shifted "from a focus on *what* we should teach to a focus on *how* the curriculum should be organized, built, and evaluated."[8] This shift in focus creates what has been called a "teacher-proof" curriculum and contributes to a kind of "de-skilling" of teachers. Instead of encouraging teachers to be prepared and willing to engage in curriculum development and knowledge-building, the teacher-proof curriculum fosters and rewards those who follow the external mandates of prepackaged, predetermined curriculum guides, textbooks, and lessons.

This chapter examines how culturally relevant teaching rejects the teacher-proof curriculum and conceives of knowledge in a broad sense.

Culturally Relevant Conceptions of Knowledge

As previously mentioned, scholars have come to recognize knowledge as a social construction. But, unfortunately, the "school knowledge" that most students experience is offered up as a given. The role and responsibility of students are merely to accept that given and reproduce it via recitation or writing. Even with the clamor for more critical thinking, memory continues to be the most rewarded skill in the nation's classrooms.[9] But culturally relevant teaching attempts to help students understand and participate in knowledge-building.

Culturally Relevant Teaching Views Knowledge as Something That Is Continuously Re-created, Recycled, and Shared

Patricia Hilliard's teaching is a model of the kind of teaching that sees knowledge as an evolutionary process (see Table 5.1). Her classroom is large and painted bright yellow and filled with evidence of student work throughout. All kinds of containers—plastic sandwich bags, plastic bowls, baskets, and boxes—hold learning objects, papers, magazines, and student folders. The classroom is filled with books, many that have an African or African American emphasis, such as *The Boy Who Didn't Believe in Spring*, by Lucille Clifton (1973), *Daydreamers*, by Eloise Greenfield (1981), and *Bringing the Rain to Kapiti Plain* (1981). Large photos above the bulletin board show such African American and Latino personalities as Nikki Giovanni, Jesse Jackson, and Cesar Chavez. The students sit in groups of four or five while working and are permitted to chat with one another in conversational tones.

Table 5.1. Conceptions of Knowledge.

Culturally Relevant	Assimilationist
Knowledge is continuously recreated, recycled, and shared by teachers and students. It is not static or unchanging.	Knowledge is static and is passed in one direction, from teacher to student.
Knowledge is viewed critically.	Knowledge is viewed as infallible.
Teacher is passionate about content.	Teacher is detached, neutral about content.
Teacher helps students develop necessary skills.	Teacher expects students to demonstrate prerequisite skills.
Teacher sees excellence as a complex standard that may involve some postulates but takes student diversity and individual differences into account.	Teacher sees excellence as a postulate that exists independently from student diversity or individual differences.

Every student in Hilliard's classroom is an author. During my classroom visits they were eager to share their latest "publications." Although she is a fan of the process-writing approach advocated by the Bay Area Writing Project, like Delpit[10] Hilliard is wary of an approach that fails to make students cognizant of the power of language and of the language of power. The process-writing approach encourages teachers and students to view writing as an ongoing process, wherein multiple drafts are written and content is valued more than writing conventions. Thus, in a first draft, students' errors in spelling, syntax, and sentence construction are not of primary import. Rather, in subsequent drafts, students are expected to improve both the form and the substance of their writing:

> I get so sick and tired of people trying to tell me that my children don't need to use any language other than the one they come to school with. Then those same people turn right around and judge the children negatively because of the way they express

themselves. My job is to make sure that they can use *both* languages, that they understand that their language is valid but that the demands placed upon them by others mean that they will constantly have to prove their worth. We spend a lot of time talking about language, what it means, how you can use it, and how it can be used against you.

Every student in my elementary school knew the words to "Lift Evr'y Voice and Sing," which we now call the black national anthem. We sang it both at school and at church. We knew that whenever we heard its plaintive opening bars, we were to stand.

At a recent Black History Month service held at the chapel of a prestigious university, I noticed that almost none of the African American students in the audience knew the black national anthem. Embarrassed, they clumsily mouthed what they thought might be the words. If it weren't so tragic, it would have been funny.

Hilliard knows how fond her students are of the rap music and hip-hop culture that pervades the radio waves and other popular media. In an attempt to help them become more at ease with standard forms of English, Hilliard asked them to vote on their favorite song. It was no surprise to her that many students selected a rap song by local hero and superstar M. C. Hammer.

I was really happy that the kids picked Hammer because some of the others are pretty rough. You know, songs filled with obscenities and negative images of women. At least I could work with some of Hammer's stuff. (She laughs.)

Hilliard copied the words of the song and distributed the text to the students the next day. The students tittered with excitement at seeing in print a song they often sang. Several began to recite it. Hilliard called for the students' attention and asked for volunteers to pronounce the rap. Three boys' hands shot up. Hilliard asked them to come to the front of the room to perform the song.

The three "rap artists" came to the front without their photocopied texts. After a brief discussion about how to begin, they "sang" (actually recited) the song, to the delight of the other students, many of whom were mouthing the words along with them. At the end of their performance there was thunderous applause from the class and the teacher alike. Hilliard thanked the boys for their willingness to share their talents. She explained that although she was their teacher and a college graduate, there was much about the song that she did not understand. She asked if the students would be willing to help her. Several laughed but all seemed willing to share their knowledge. Hilliard placed a transparency of the lyrics on the overhead projector. She had double-spaced the copy so that she could write between the lines. She explained to the students that they would be doing what interpreters do when they translate from one language into another.

Line by line the students went through the rap lyrics and explained what they meant. Hilliard carefully transferred their informal words into a more standard form. From time to time she placed words in a vocabulary list. Although she did not ask them to, most of the students copied Hilliard's version to their own papers. After the class, Hilliard explained her goals for this activity.

> We'll continue doing this kind of thing all year long. I want the children to see that they have some valuable knowledge to contribute. I don't want them to be ashamed of what they know but I also want them to know and be comfortable with what school and the rest of the society requires. When I put it in the context of "translation" they get excited. They see it is possible to go from one to the other. It's not that they are not familiar with Standard English . . . they hear Standard English all the time on TV. It's certainly what I use in the classroom. But there is rarely any connection made between the way they speak and Standard English. I think that when they can see the connections and know that they can make the shifts, they become better at both. They're bilingual!

This notion of speakers of African American language as bilingual is a decidedly different perspective. It overlaps with the discussion in Chapter Three about teachers' perceptions of students. By believing her students to be capable and knowledgeable, Hilliard reinforces this belief and her high expectations for the students. The language they bring with them serves as a tool that helps them with additional language learning, just as speakers of Standard English use English to help them acquire new languages.

In Ann Lewis's sixth-grade class, knowledge construction is a full-time activity. Ann paid close attention to the debate about the state's new history and social science curricula. One area of contention, the diluting of multicultural issues and concerns, was of special interest to Lewis. Because the state curricula would determine which books were available to teachers, she knew that she and her students could not rely on these books alone and would have to develop their own social studies program. She decided to analyze one of the questions that emerged from the curriculum debate with her students: Were the ancient Egyptians black?

On a large piece of paper, Lewis wrote out the question. She divided the paper into two sections. On one side she wrote, "Confirming Evidence." On the other side she wrote, "Disconfirming Evidence." The titles were consistent with her practice of using sophisticated vocabulary with her students.

She explained to the students that they would be conducting research in order to answer the question of the ancient Egyptians' race.

Lewis: Why would we care whether or not the Egyptians were black?

First student: Because then we could prove that black people did great things.

Lewis: But can't we already prove that black people did great things? Don't we already know about a lot of black people who have done great things?

Second student: Yeah, but you know how they're always talkin'
about great things from Europe and how all these white
people did so many great things, but you never hear
about great things from Africa. They talk about Egypt
but they talk about it like it's not Africa.

Lewis: Why do you think that's so?

Second student: Well, because everybody can see the great things
the Egyptians did, like the pyramids, so then if you just
talk about Egypt maybe people won't think about it as a
part of Africa.

Third student: What does that prove?

Second student: I didn't say it proved anything. I'm just sayin' that
if you make people think of the Egyptians as white then
you will think that only white people can make great
things.

The discussion continued as many of the students expressed
their opinions about ancient Egypt. Some referred to movies they
had seen depicting ancient Egyptians as white. Almost all of the
students had seen *Cleopatra* and *The Ten Commandments*.

Lewis encouraged the students to raise additional questions,
which she wrote on the board. By the end of the discussion, she
had a series of student comments and questions that she wanted
them to investigate in order to answer the initial question.
Next, she asked the students to suggest ways that they could find
the answers to these questions. The students suggested library
research, interviews of experts, educational films. She asked each
team of five or six students (there were five teams in the class) to
select a question and discuss how they would divide their work
and start their investigation.

The quest to answer the question about the ancient Egyptians'
race went on for almost a month. In the second week, one of the
teams decided that the class should identify itself as the "Imhotep
Project." In the course of its research, this team had discovered

Imhotep, the first physician known by name, later elevated to the status of a god.

As a result of this month-long inquiry Lewis's students probably learned much more than they would have from a textbook lesson about ancient Egypt. And, although they did not settle the question conclusively, they felt that the evidence they assembled supporting the blackness of the ancient Egyptians was more compelling than that refuting it.

An interesting point about the students' classroom experience is that, in larger society's debate about multiculturalism, conservative scholars have suggested that knowing the race or ethnicity of historical figures does little to enhance the learning of students of color. (This would probably be true if all teachers did was to recite a laundry list of people of color—tangential to the "real" history.) But by making race problematic, Lewis helped the students understand that knowledge is not something hidden in a book. Rather than require the students to remember and recite some predetermined facts about ancient Egypt, she led them on an adventure toward answering a question that is important to students of color.

In the course of that quest, the students learned many other things about the ancient civilization. They learned why it was regarded as a great civilization. They raised their own questions about ancient Egypt. They confronted contradictory information and learned that even the experts disagree sometimes.

Stately and dignified, my Black History professor strolled into the college classroom. He was a man of international reknown, having written many books about the African American participation in the shaping of the United States. For sixty minutes every Monday, Wednesday, and Friday, we sat enraptured as the greatness of Africans and African Americans unfolded for us. Why had it taken us so long to learn this? What about all that stuff taught in high school? Were my African American high school classmates who had not gone on to a college that taught these truths condemned to a life of believing that their people had never made anything, had never done anything, are nothing?

A hallmark of the culturally relevant notion of knowledge is that it is something that each student brings to the classroom. Students are not seen as empty vessels to be filled by all-knowing teachers. What they know is acknowledged, valued, and incorporated into the classroom.

A common theme in all of my interviews with the teachers in my study was an acknowledgment of how much the students know.

Pauline Dupree recognizes the link between verbal ability and cognition. Rather than concern herself solely with the form of students' language, she is interested in the meaning and sense of their words.

> Our children are very verbal and very bright. They can really get going on a topic and make you think about it in so many different ways.

Gertrude Winston expresses frustration at the limits of standardized testing in measuring student knowledge accurately. Rather than being concerned about memorization of trivial or out-of-context information, she acknowledges the complexity of students' knowledge. This sensitivity to their knowledge and skills reflects her belief system and can be seen in the high expectations she holds for her students.

> Nobody ever really measures what the children really know. They have knowledge and skills that don't show up on standardized tests—important knowledge and skills, the kind of stuff that can mean the difference between life and death.

Ann Lewis's words are filled with anger about the ultimate future of the students in the district. Seeing extremely bright elementary school children fail in high school fires her political consciousness; she has seen for herself that the students are capable.

> I've worked with children in this school who were geniuses. I mean it, geniuses, minds so quick you wouldn't believe, able to conceptualize in ways far beyond college professors I've had. I just can't reconcile their intelligence with what happens to them in high school (where there is a 70 percent drop-out rate of students from this district).

For Lewis, the students' performance in school is less related to their family structure, their income, or their race, than it is to their ability to receive quality education. However, she has enough political savvy to know that the combination of student status and race with structural inequalities can mean educational failure. She believes that teachers should play an intervening role between the students' lives and the society.

Like Ann Lewis, Patricia Hilliard recognizes the powerful negative impact poor schooling has on students like hers. She is able to identify their intellectual strengths and motivations while simultaneously recognizing the ways that much of their schooling has served to demotivate them.

> I've taught all kinds of kids, rich ones, poor ones, white ones, black ones. Some of the smartest youngsters I've worked with have been right here in this community, but a lot of the time they don't believe in themselves. School saps the life out of them. You want to see intelligence walking around on two legs? Just go into a kindergarten class. They come to school with fresh faces, full of wonder. But by third grade you can see how badly school has beaten them down. You can really see it in the boys. I sometimes ask myself just what it is we're doing to these children.

Elizabeth Harris's spiritual and religious convictions demand that she see every child's potential. Her concern with fairness and justice is rooted in her Christianity. For her, working with the children is a "holy" responsibility and her adherence to the golden rule is unwavering.

> God's little flowers, that's what I call them. Everyone a little different but everyone so sweet. And just like a garden, the classroom has got to be a place that nurtures them. They don't all need the same thing. One might need a little more sunlight, another a little fertilizer. Some might need a little pruning (she laughs) and some might need to roam free. They're just so precious and it breaks my heart to see the hurtful way they are treated. Some teachers think they are hard because they live tough lives but they are just as fragile as hothouse orchids.

Margaret Rossi's broader social analysis is reflected in her dialectical relationship with her students. Rossi understands that her future is inextricably linked with that of her students. By ensuring their success, she reasons, she ensures her own. Perhaps her training as a nun gave her an ethical perspective grounded in religious practice like that of Elizabeth Harris.

> I can't think of anything any one of my students could do to keep me from teaching them. If more teachers understood the connection between themselves and their students they might feel this same way. These children are the future. There is no way for me to have a secure future if they don't have one. It's going to take three of them to support one of me in my retirement years. They have to be capable of assuming highly skilled positions. They have the brain power, but they need the opportunity. The society can't keep saying, "I'm sorry but there's no place for you." I'm amazed that we don't see more rage among African Americans.

These teachers' belief in the knowledge their students bring to school is quite different from the view of African American students revealed by a set of comments I collected in a predominately white school district:

How can I hook these unmotivated, uninterested, low-achieving African American children who have no vision of a future in the world of employment? These children are usually from poor, disadvantaged families on welfare assistance.

A lot of African American children come from homes with little structure, discipline, and value for education. The deck is already stacked against them.

Most of the black students come from this neighborhood. It has a very poor reputation and a history of problems. What insights do you have about dealing with students from this neighborhood?

These students generally lack that "spark" for learning because of all these environmental factors—parental neglect, abuse.... I'm not just referring to one or two kids in my room but close to 50 percent of my classroom.

We need help accepting black children's differences which are so drastically different from the white upper-class students who also attend this school.

Although these statements represent a cross section of teacher responses, I do not believe they are atypical. After conducting scores of teacher workshops and teacher education classes throughout the country, I have heard similar beliefs expressed. In the case of these teachers' statements, I have the added advantage of knowing the community (and the community members) that they are discussing. The teachers and I read the students' circumstances very differently. The teachers seem to see only deficit and need. I admire the resilience and strength of the students who continue to come to school and participate, even when their intellect and culture are regularly questioned.

These kinds of statements underscore the deep ideological biases and lack of expectations for success for African American students that exist for too many teachers.[11] As a researcher I am cynical about the potential for change. But as an African American parent I am desperate for change. I cling to the possibilities held forth by culturally relevant teaching.

Culturally Relevant Teaching Views Knowledge Critically

Ann Lewis's Imhotep Project, discussed earlier in this chapter, is a good example of the kind of teaching that views knowledge critically. An example from Julia Devereaux's class also illustrates this view.

Devereaux resembles a perpetual-motion machine and her class reflects her "busy-ness." An early morning visitor sees students going about various management tasks. One is taking the roll, another collecting lunch money, still another collecting permission slips for an upcoming field trip. Once the late bell rings, Devereaux forces herself to sit down and then asks rhetorically, "What should we do today?"

On one particular day, when the students had finished reading a Greek myth about a princess, Devereaux asked, "How would you describe the princess?" Her question was designed to elicit responses about the princess's character, but the first student to respond began with a physical description. "She was beautiful, with long blond hair," said the student. Nowhere in the story was there a description that matched this response. "What makes you say that?" Devereaux asked. "Because that's the way princesses always are," the student replied. "I don't have long blond hair and neither does anyone else in here. Does that mean that none of us could be a princess?" Devereaux asked. The student and several others seemed resigned to the fact that that was the case. Devereaux feigned disbelief that they were unaware of black princesses.

Slowly, without fanfare, Devereaux walked to her bookshelf and selected a book, John Steptoe's *Mufaro's Beautiful Daughters* (1987), about two African sisters, one good and one evil. After reading the fourth graders the book, Devereaux asked how many students still believed that a princess had to have long blond hair. No one raised a hand.

In our discussion after class, Devereaux told me that she had not intended to read that book.

> I just couldn't believe that in this day and age our children still believe that white skin and long blond hair is the standard of beauty. When that child said that I thought I would have a stroke. It just goes to show you how powerful the things they see and hear are. People think we're nit-picking when we talk about needing materials that include people who resemble the students. I realize we were reading a Greek myth, and that's a whole other story, but the students have got to be able to ask, "Is this the truth? Whose reality is this?"

Devereaux's spontaneous dismay about the students' images of princesses is the kind of reaction that teachers must have in order to respond critically to the content students are presented in the classroom. The ability to create knowledge works in conjunction with the ability (and the need) to be critical of content.

Margaret Rossi learned a way to help her students develop their critical capacity from a lesson she read about in the radical education newspaper, *Rethinking Schools*. One afternoon, just before the social studies period, Rossi sent one of her students on an errand to the teacher next door. While the student was gone, Rossi sat at her desk. When she returned, Rossi exclaimed, "Look at all this great stuff *I discovered* in this desk *I discovered!*" Rossi began raving over the pencils, books, and other personal effects in the student's desk, which she now claimed as her own. "Uh-un, Ms. Rossi. You know you wrong!" the student exclaimed, her hands on her hips. The rest of the class laughed uproariously as Rossi and the student argued back and forth about the ownership of the desk. Finally, Rossi gave up the desk and went to the chalkboard where she wrote the word "discover."

In the subsequent discussion, the students contended that a person could not be said to have "discovered" something that belonged to others. At this point, Rossi asked the students to turn to a section of their social studies textbook (which bore the copyright date 1977) entitled, "The Age of Discovery." Rossi posed a series of questions about the European explorers. Her students also raised questions. Gradually, their textbook took on a less authoritative aura. Rossi seemed pleased with the way the lesson developed.

> I didn't ask LaShondra to act out that scene about my discovering her desk, but she was wonderful. I had read about a teacher who did something similar with high school students in Oregon and I knew that my students could handle this. Last year in fifth grade most of them learned the Columbus "mantra" so I wanted them to really think about this idea of "discovery" as we study world history. My kids are naturally skeptical because their lives don't match what they see on TV or in their textbooks. I have to work to make sure they understand that it's okay for them to challenge what's in the book. It should be simple for them, but like kids everywhere they want to accept the book as gospel. Now they know that will never do. (She laughs.)

The ability to examine critically and challenge knowledge is not a mere classroom exercise. By drawing on the perspectives of critical theorists, culturally relevant teaching attempts to make

knowledge problematic. Students are challenged to view education (and knowledge) as a vehicle for emancipation, to understand the significance of their cultures, and to recognize the
power of language.[12] As a matter of course, culturally relevant
teaching makes a link between classroom experiences and the
students' everyday lives. These connections are made in spirited
discussions and classroom interactions. Teachers are not afraid to
assume oppositional viewpoints to foster the students' confidence
in challenging what may be inaccurate or problematic.

By explicitly laying the ground rules for debate and creating a
psychologically safe place, this kind of teaching allows students
to express themselves in a variety of forms (for example, in their
conversation, in their writing, in their art). By owning the form of
expression, students become enthusiastic participants in classroom
discourse and activities. This spiritedness is reflected in the next
characteristic of the culturally relevant concept of knowledge.

Culturally Relevant Teaching Is Passionate About Knowledge

For several years I served on university interview panels for education candidates. Because of the renewed popularity of teaching
as a career and because of the reputation of our teacher education
program, and its small size, we received applications from many
more than we had spaces for. We decided that each candidate
should come in for an interview. Although the interviews rarely
excluded a candidate who met the admission requirements,
they sometimes served to improve the chances of a student who
seemed marginal on paper. Generally the interviews confirmed
what was already evident in a candidate's file.

One of the first questions asked of each candidate was, "Why
do you want to be a teacher?" A stock answer for prospective elementary teachers was, "I just love kids." It also was not unusual
to hear someone say something to the effect that she (and it was
almost always women who applied to the elementary education

program) "got along better with kids than with adults." Along with my fellow teacher education professionals, I believe that caring about youngsters is an important prerequisite for a teaching career. However, after a couple of years of hearing, "I just love kids," we began to respond, "Yes, but why do you want to *teach?*" We suggested to candidates that they could choose many careers other than teaching and still "be with kids." We suggested such professions as pediatrics or pediatric nursing, library science, recreation, or social work.

Most of the candidates were at a loss when asked to explain further why they wanted to teach. Some commented that they had loved school or that they were from a family of teachers. I cannot recall a single one who talked about loving intellectual activity or who spoke of knowledge as empowering. Of course, this may have been a function of their youth and inexperience. However, a colleague who had taught many of the prospective students in the college of arts and sciences remarked, "The very students who hate learning and intellectual rigor seem to be the ones who decide they want to teach."

Shulman reminds us:

> Teaching is, essentially, a learned profession. A teacher is a member of a scholarly community. He or she must understand the structures of subject matter, the principles of conceptual organization, and the principles of inquiry that help answer two kinds of questions in each field: What are the important ideas and skills in this domain? And how are new ideas added and deficient ones dropped by those who produce knowledge in this area? That is, what are the rules and procedures of good scholarship or inquiry?[13]

A search for important ideas and the construction of knowledge fuels the excitement and enthusiasm that exemplify culturally relevant teaching. For example, instead of concentrating on memorizing facts, such as the names of their U.S. senators and representatives, students are encouraged to think about the ways that these officials function in relation to their constituents. Thus the teachers help the students conceive of analogies that make this relationship understandable. In one instance, Rossi talked to the students about the governing structure of a Baptist church, with the pastor as president, the deacons as senators, and the trustees as representatives. Within a few minutes, students were able to demonstrate a rudimentary knowledge of how the two houses of Congress work. The important idea was that in a bicameral legislative body, the two houses are chosen differently, have different functions, and wield different power. Just knowing the names of congresspeople does not imply creating knowledge.

Culturally Relevant Teaching Helps Students Develop Necessary Skills

By building bridges or a scaffolding that meets students where they are (intellectually and functionally), culturally relevant teaching helps them to be where they need to be to participate fully and meaningfully in the construction of knowledge. In contrast, assimilationist teaching assumes that students come to class with certain skills and suggests that it is impossible to teach those who are not at a certain skill level.

As one teacher noted, "There is a curious phenomenon occurring in schools today. Teachers expect students to come to school reading and they resent those children who don't. If that's the case, what do they need a teacher for?"

Margaret Rossi's thinking about her students' abilities is a good example of the bridge-building quality in action. Despite the mandated curriculum, Rossi regularly challenges her sixth-grade students with algebra. Although many previously have been unsuccessful in mathematics, Rossi takes an approach that says they can and will learn the sophisticated mathematical ideas and concepts of algebra. Rather than select the top students to participate, Rossi expects the entire class to develop competency in algebra—both problem-solving and problem-posing abilities. Even James, a student whom previous teachers have described as special-education material, is included in these sessions.

Rather than place James in a special group or attempt "to keep him busy" with sheets of drill (and kill) problems, Rossi works hard to build on the skills he already has and helps him make connections to the new learning. By providing him with a few structural clues, she builds his confidence, allowing him the psychological freedom to solve some problems and raise questions. His inclusion in the sessions also means that students with more advanced skills have the opportunity to act as teachers without regarding him as capable only of "baby work."

Gertrude Winston also builds bridges and scaffolding for her students. However, she gets the help of parents and other adults as she does so. The following example is representative of Winston's shared-responsibility strategy:

Like most ten-year-olds in the United States, Winston's fifth graders cannot imagine life without television. This semester, Winston uses their natural curiosity about how things were "way back when" to look at leisure time during the late 1700s and early 1800s. One of the participatory activities she offers is a quilting bee.

Winston calls upon parents and grandparents to come demonstrate their skills with needle and thread to help make the class quilt; even small children are allowed. The quilting bee becomes an intergenerational affair.

Winston points out that in the past older siblings were regularly asked to care for younger ones. She also helps her students make connections between quilting and the kind of crafts that African slaves brought with them to this country.

On the day of the quilting bee, Winston's class looks very different. The students' tables are pushed to one side of the room, and their chairs are arranged in a big circle around the room. Winston wants to create a feeling of a big family, where everyone can see everyone else and talk not only to the people seated near them but also across the circle. Adults bring covered dishes to share.

Students take turns watching the younger children. Some parents come only for an hour or two because of other commitments. Some who can't come were asked to send along a special dish or eventually do some of the finishing work on the quilt (such as hemming or ironing). Finally, never one to waste a resource, Winston has her students identify a charity or a needy family to which the finished quilt will be donated.

Several reading and writing activities are associated with this activity; overall, the activity helps the students to use and improve the skills they had and to learn new ones. One student's journal reads:

> No wonder the people of old times didn't need no TV. They were so busy with their work that they didn't have no time to just sit and watch a TV. If you wanted to make a quilt you could have a lot of people over and talk and visit and eat. It's like having a party but you get your work done. My Auntie did something like that when she moved to a new house. Our hole (sic) family was there to help her clean and paint. We had a lot of food and we got the work done fast because we had a lot of help.

This journal entry demonstrates the ways that Winston's integrative and communal approach fosters basic skills like literacy. And by situating the learning in a context that includes the families and even serves the community in a small way, she makes a strong connection between knowledge and power.

Finally, Culturally Relevant Teaching Sees Excellence as a Complex Standard That Takes Student Diversity and Individual Differences into Account

Each of the classrooms I studied were examples of this characteristic. However, for the purpose of explanation I will focus on those of Pauline Dupree and Peggy Valentine.

Dupree's classroom structure might cause the casual observer to dismiss her teaching as too regimented, too authoritarian. However, after ongoing and in-depth observations the reason her style can be considered culturally relevant becomes apparent. Always on the lookout for ways to recognize and affirm student accomplishments, Dupree distinguishes between acknowledging student effort and rewarding substandard performance:

> I don't believe in telling students that they are doing well when they aren't. Some teachers come into this district and think they're doing the children a favor by sticking a star on everything. They don't care that they're rewarding mediocrity. But in doing so, they're really just setting the kids up for failure because somewhere down the road they're going to learn that that A was really a C or a D.

> What I try to do is find those things the children really are good at and acknowledge them in the classroom. That means knowing about their sports and church activities. If someone is on a championship team, we try to get the coach to come in and talk about that person's contribution. I have had coaches, ministers, Scout leaders, family members—you name it—in here to tell the class about the excellence of the class members.

Dupree's in-class recognition of out-of-class excellence encourages the students to conceive of excellence broadly. It also begins to create a stronger connection between home and school. Once students see that Dupree makes a fuss about the things they enjoy, they seek similar recognition in the classroom.

Valentine's approach to acknowledging a broad range of student excellence involves the students in making the assessment. Each week during a class meeting the students nominate classmates for excellence in a variety of areas, both academic and social. Each nomination is supported by evidence. To ensure that the nominations are sincere, Valentine asks students to substantiate them orally. For example, "I nominate Tyrell for an excellence award because he helped me with my math this week." Other members of the class are encouraged to question the nomination. Valentine allows extracurricular activities as a basis for nomination but pushes students to think about classroom and school-related deeds by reminding them that the nominations have a better chance of success when others can verify them. After the nominations have been made, the students take a vote. Valentine rewards the winner with a small prize or privilege: Gift certificates for the local fast food outlet, extended recess time, and exemptions from particular assignments are examples.

In addition to the weekly excellence awards, Valentine has her students participate in an "internship program." She pairs students with workers in the school such as the janitor, a secretary, the library aide, cafeteria workers, and teachers' aides, so that they get a brief opportunity to learn about the value of work. According to Valentine:

> Fewer and fewer of our students understand the value of work or see work as a productive and satisfying activity. Too many of the teenagers won't take jobs in fast food stores because they don't pay much and because their friends would tease them. Because you can make easy money on the street, kids think anybody who takes a job at a fast food place is a fool. With the internship I'm just trying to get the kids to see that we work for more than money. We work because our work means something to us.

Thus culturally relevant teaching recognizes the need for students to experience excellence without deceiving them about their own academic achievement. Rewarding students for a wide array of activities ensures that they understand that hard-and-fast rules do not exist for determining excellence. It also underscores the students' understanding that the teacher has high expectations for each of them.

On a cold day in late January, five of my African American class-mates and I sat together at a post–junior high school graduation celebra-tion that we had planned for ourselves. We had attended the obligatory school-sponsored affair, but months earlier we had promised ourselves that we would have a private party where we could congratulate each other and be ourselves. We felt we deserved this—we had all survived 9A-1 and 9B-1, the college preparatory Latin sections.

Two of the boys, Sam Fortune and Larry Allen, were going to attend the all-boys, academically challenging Central High School. A third boy, Carlton Epps, would attend Bartram High School, the high school within the geographical boundary of our junior high. His mother wanted to keep him on the "right track." One of the girls, Carol Oglesby, was going on to vocational school. She was tired of trying to prove herself to white teachers and students. Another girl, Sandra Webb, and I were going on to Overbrook High School, a school that was racially mixed because of its location, which bordered both an African American community and a Jewish one. Sandra was going to follow the school's commercial course track. I remained in an honors program and took another two years of Latin.

I had graduated from a junior high school that I hated with straight A's. I had had a report card of straight A's and I was miserable. I had not earned those A's because I was smart. I had not earned them because I wanted to be an outstanding student. I had earned them because my teachers did not think I could earn them and I had vowed right then and there to live up to my own standards of excellence.

Concluding Thoughts

In Chapters Three, Four, and Five, I attempted to outline the characteristics of culturally relevant teaching by providing class-room vignettes and teacher observations. In the next chapter, I will look at these characteristics in the context of the subject matter taught in classrooms.

By examining the teaching of such basic skills as reading and math I will attempt to situate culturally relevant teaching in contexts that are familiar to and comfortable for most elementary school teachers. Also, doing this is an attempt to transform the concept into "knowledge in use"—to move it from the theoretical and conceptual to the practical.

* 6 *

Culturally Relevant Teaching

Hold fast to dreams
For if dreams die
Life is a broken winged butterfly....

—LANGSTON HUGHES

Chapters Three through Five offered a look at culturally relevant teaching practices through teacher interviews and classroom observations. In this chapter I offer a more contextualized examination of the activities of four classrooms, three in which culturally relevant teaching was practiced and one in which it was not. The context for two of the classes is a reading lesson and for the other classes it is a math lesson.

The Focus on Literacy

One of the critical national indicators of educational progress (and national development) is the literacy rate. Amove and Graff assert that national literacy campaigns are not unique to the twentieth century; many charismatic leaders have used literacy campaigns for "salvation, redemption, and re-creation." They suggest that in the twentieth century, especially since 1960, "literacy has been seen as a process of consciousness-raising aimed at human

---

The epigraph on this page is from *The Panther and the Lash* by Langston Hughes. Copyright 1951 by Langston Hughes. Reprinted by permission of Alfred A. Knopf, Inc. and Harold Ober Associates Incorporated.

liberation."[1] National literacy campaigns have been a part of the social and political fabric of such countries as Brazil, Cuba, and Guineau Bissau. However, the aim of literacy campaigns in the United States has been individual and personal advancement. Nightly public service messages on television exhort citizens to sign up at local libraries and schools for reading instruction. An explanation of this trend is presented by Ferdman: "In a society tending toward homogeneity, it is easy to think of literacy simply in terms of specific skills and activities. Given broad cultural consensus on the definition of literacy, alternative constructions are either remote or invisible, and so literacy becomes a seemingly self-evident personal attribute that is either present or absent."[2] But Ferdman further contends that in a multiethnic society the "cultural framework" for literacy must be considered. Thus in citing deCastell and Luke,[3] Ferdman points out that "being literate has always referred to having mastery over the processes by means of which culturally significant information is coded."

The following passage is central to Ferdman's argument: "In a culturally heterogeneous society, literacy ceases to be a characteristic inherent solely in the individual. It becomes an interactive process that is constantly redefined and renegotiated, as the individual transacts with the socioculturally fluid surroundings."

In the context of this study of culturally relevant teaching, the construction of literacy among African Americans is especially important. Gadsden contends: "For African American learners, in particular, literacy has been an especially tenuous struggle, from outright denial during slavery, to limited access in the early 1900s, to segregated schools with often outdated textbooks well into the 1960s, to—many might argue—marginal acceptance of their culture and capacity as learners even into the 1990s."[4]

My father completed only about four years of formal schooling. His school was a one-room classroom that he, his four brothers, and his two sisters attended. By the time my father was in what was considered to be fourth grade, he had learned as much as his older siblings who had stopped attending school to help with farming chores at home. In an attempt to escape the harsh discipline of his stepmother when he was about twelve years old, he and an older brother ran away from home to live with an adult sister in Philadelphia. By the time he arrived, school was but a distant memory. He kept up his reading with the newspaper every day and the Bible every night.

When I reached junior high school, my father would thumb through my textbooks and read them as if he actually found them interesting.

The next section of this chapter describes culturally relevant literacy instruction in Ann Lewis's and Julia Devereaux's classrooms. They make literacy a communal activity and demonstrate ways to make learning to read and write a more meaningful and successful enterprise for African American learners.

Ann Lewis: A Literacy Revival

In Chapter Three, I provided a "snapshot" view of Ann Lewis. To reiterate, Lewis is an Italian American woman in her midforties. Active in school and community politics, she has lived most of her life in the largely African American community where she teaches. Some of the older teachers and administrators in the district were her teachers. Lewis remembers herself as less than an ideal student:

> I grew up in the community and my greatest desire was to teach here, basically because I spent so much time with quality teachers and those teachers encouraged me to teach. As strict as those teachers were with me, they pushed me to do what was right. I was a difficult child in class and that's why I started teaching— to give other so-called difficult children a real chance.

Lewis did not take a traditional route to teaching. Having married soon after high school, she began her adult life as a homemaker, mother, and wife. But the breakup of her marriage meant that she needed to work to support herself and her children. She secured a job as a teacher's aide in a local elementary school. Her decision to work in the schools came in the early 1970s, at a time when schools and school districts described as economically disadvantaged received additional state and federal funds to hire community people, particularly parents, as paraprofessionals. Familiarity with both the school and the home culture made the teachers' aides a special resource. Students and parents who were intimidated by the formality and cultural barriers between themselves and the school's more formal staff often sought out the teachers' aides for assistance and support.

Aware that teachers' aides were an important resource and that turnover among the teaching staff was on the increase, the school district proposed and implemented a program to encourage the aides to attend the local community college, transfer to the state university, and then enroll in the university's fifth year teacher accreditation program. With a critical mass of teachers' aides enrolling in the program, the district, in conjunction with the community college, could offer courses in the school district so that the aides were able to keep their jobs. Lewis was among the first group of aides to take advantage of the program.

Although many aides enthusiastically began the district-sponsored program, time and circumstances kept most from completing it. Lewis was one of the few who endured and completed it. She began as a certified teacher in the district in 1977.

By 1983 Lewis had built a reputation in the school district for her assertive, even aggressive, advocacy of teachers' rights. She had been elected president of the teachers' association and was a self-appointed watchdog for the school board, attending every meeting and taking public issue with positions she felt were not in the best interests of the teachers. Not known for her diplomacy or tact, she often locked horns with board members and school administrators about what she perceived as violations of the teachers' contract. This kind of behavior is risky in a small district such as Pinewood, where board members and district administrators can have an inordinate amount of influence on the day-to-day running of the school. Lewis felt that, perhaps because they shared the feelings of board members and district administrators, or because they saw it as a way to ingratiate themselves with their superiors, her principals attempted to apply subtle forms of harassment. She received many of the students that no other teacher wanted. I suggested to Lewis that maybe these students were assigned to her because of a principal's confidence in her ability to work with them, whereas her colleagues could not. Lewis gave me a look indicating that I might be out of touch with the reality of urban schools.

In the spring of 1983 Lewis seriously rethought her decision to teach. She knew she still loved being in the classroom. Further, because of her reputation as an excellent teacher, many parents requested (and even demanded) that their children be placed in her class. Thus administrative attempts to stack her class with "trouble-makers" were thwarted by these concerned parents who saw that Lewis offered a special intellectual opportunity for their children. But she was weary of her battles with the district and school board. She felt as if she were working two jobs; and her "night job" was affecting her performance on her "day job."

One piece of good fortune for Lewis was a friendship with a colleague who had gone on to become an administrator in the district. Now a principal, her friend told Lewis about the Bay Area Writing Project and suggested that Lewis and another teacher take advantage of the seven-week program, which was offered at the University of California at Berkeley. Because none of her other colleagues were interested in giving up seven weeks of their summer, Lewis faced no competition for the scholarship offered.

Today Lewis credits this experience with renewing her enthusiasm for teaching:

> I can't tell you how that experience changed me. It's not so much that the philosophy was radical or revolutionary. In fact, it was

kind of like a recognition that the way I thought about teaching was all right. It was the intellectual activity, you know, the
thinking. Because I wasn't bombarding my kids with worksheets,
I think some of the other teachers thought I wasn't working
hard. But I was trying to get at their thinking, to remind them
that they *could* think, that thinking was allowed in school.
I came back here in the fall and totally restructured my class
around writing (and later literature) and I had the research to
back it up.

When my study began, Lewis was in the seventh year of her
revised curriculum. Each year and each class of fifth or sixth graders brought new permutations to her ideas and her thinking about
the kind of education the community required.

During the first year of my observations, I visited Lewis's sixth-
grade class regularly but randomly, that is, I went there every
week but at varied times. I felt that appearing at different times
helped me to see the different moods of the classroom.

Fall 1990 marked the second year of Lewis's participation in
the study. In this second year I began to appear at a set time each
week. Although Lewis's teaching was not circumscribed by a pre-
dictable schedule (of reading, math, science, and so on) literacy
teaching was more likely in the mornings. My field notes describe
my first visit that year:

> I arrived at the school at 8:45 on Thursday morning. The school
> grounds were quiet. I noticed that the lawn was freshly cut, a
> sure sign of the beginning of the school year. I stopped at the
> main office to sign in and speak to the principal. The secretary
> informed me that the principal was covering a class because they
> had been unable to get a substitute. As I walked through the
> inner courtyard I noticed the vice principal talking with two
> black girls who looked to be about twelve years old. He seemed
> to be reprimanding—or perhaps counseling—them. The noise

level of the class next to Ann Lewis's was high. Students were talking, the teacher was shouting. I noticed the contrast when I walked into Ann's class, which was unusually quiet. The students were listening as one of them read aloud.

The class was studying *Charlie Pippin* by Candi Dawson Boyd. [The novel] is about an eleven-year-old African American girl who attempts to win the approval of her father, a decorated Vietnam War veteran who has buried all his feelings about the war within him. The girl feels alienated from her father and wants to find a way to reach him. Ann and her students were about twenty pages into the book.

There were twenty-nine students in the class (twenty African Americans). When the student who was reading finished, an African American boy, Jerry, asked, "Is she [the story's protagonist] going to stay eleven years old in this book?"

Lewis responded with a question, "What about in *Driving Miss Daisy?* Did the main character stay the same age?"

Students (in unison): "No."

Ann: "How do you know?"

Jerry: "Because she was using one of those walkin' things when she got old."

Ann: "A walker?"

Jerry: "Yeah, and then she was in the old folks home."

Ann: "Can you see without a video?"

Calvin (another African American boy): "Yes, you can see when you're reading. So we'll see how old Charlie is in the book!"

Ann reminded the students about a previous discussion about "connotation" and "denotation" and said, "Remember we said 'hungry' makes you think one way but 'famished' makes you think another way?"

Calvin asked if the discussion could go back to talking about the book and Ann encouraged him. "She got feelings her dad doesn't understand and he got feelings she don't understand."

Ann: "Do you know anybody who ever feels like this?"
Calvin: "Me!"

Ann drew a Venn diagram to represent similarities and differences between Calvin and the character in the story. "You have your own video of your entire life in your head. Every time you read, you can get an image of how the story connects with your life. Do you want to get back to the story?"

"Yeah!" the class says in unison.

A third boy began to read. When he finished, Lewis said, "Close your eyes. Let's put on your video." She then re-read a section of the book describing the mother in the story. "How can you relate this to your life?" One of the African American girls commented "That's just like when I kiss my mom."

Students took turns reading passages from the book. For some, this was the first "chapter" book they'd read in school. Some of these slower readers had trouble with some of the words. Lewis encouraged them and urged other class members to help. "Remember, we're all a team here. We've got to help each other." When Charlene (an African American girl) asked a question about a dispute the main character had with her father, Lewis suggested the students role-play to understand better. Two students struggled a bit with the role-play. Two others gave it a try and got a round of applause from the rest of the class.

After the role-play Ann asked, "What do we know about Charlie's dad?" The class erupted with excitement—many wanted to contribute. Lewis began to develop a "character-attribute web" on the board. As the students became more excited, she encouraged them to settle down by explaining which part of the brain they were using. "We're not in the limbic [she pointed to a bulletin-board diagram of the brain], we're in the cerebellum. Let's not deteriorate into reptilian. Okay, you now have two minutes to talk with someone about other attributes of Charlie's dad."

When the two minutes were up, many students contributed to the attribute web. Ann filled the board with the student responses and shouted, "That was perfect! You're a *perfect* class. If you're perfect raise your hand!" Twenty-nine hands were in the air.

Over the course of the next several months, *Charlie Pippin* became the centerpiece for a wide range of activities. One group of students began a Vietnam War research group. One group member who assumed a leadership position was a very quiet Vietnamese girl whose relatives had fought in the war. She brought in pictures, maps, letters, even a family member to talk to the class about Vietnam. In the book, the main character—Charlie—had made origami to sell to her classmates. Lewis taught her students how to make origami. She introduced them to Eleanor Coerr's *Sadako and the Thousand Paper Cranes*. A second group of students researched nuclear proliferation. They asked Lewis to rent the video "Amazing Grace," which is about a young boy's and a professional athlete's stand against nuclear weapons. The entire study took place against the backdrop of an impending war between the United States and its allies and Iraq.

Several of the students decided that, like Sadako, they could make paper cranes to symbolize their opposition to war. In a way, the students believed that their efforts might even prevent the war. Although Lewis gave them no extra time to make their cranes, they found many opportunities to do so. By January 15, the date that then-President George Bush had set to move into Kuwait, Lewis's class had folded and hung up in their classroom window 1,039 paper cranes—tiny paper birds that stood as a symbol of their commitment to peace.

It is interesting to note that Lewis's reference to the parts of the brain, and later class discussions about learning taxonomies, grew out of her own experiences at that time: She was taking a graduate course and shared much of her learning and experiences with the students. She brought readings and the language from her graduate studies into her sixth-grade classroom. The students seemed eager to hear about what she was learning and to enjoy the vision of her as a student and of themselves as "graduate students."

Thus during this year I witnessed a class of students engaged in reading, writing, and speaking activities with increasing levels of competence and confidence. One of the hallmarks of Lewis's class was the intellectual leadership demonstrated by the African American boys. Although most of them had had previous problems, including poor academic performance, truancy, suspensions, recommendation for special-education placement, and at least one threatened expulsion, Lewis's class represented an opportunity for a new academic beginning.

One of Lewis's star students, a boy named Larry, had had a particularly troubling history. Although he was short and slightly built, he was the oldest child in the class. He had been left back several times and was thirteen in a class made up of eleven-year-olds. He had been traumatized by the drive-by shooting of a favorite aunt. Other teachers in the school referred to him as "an accident just waiting to happen." None wanted him in their classrooms. Lewis referred to Larry as "a piece of crystal."

> He's strong and beautiful but fragile. I have to build a safe and secure place for him and let him know that we—the class and I—will be here for him. The school has been placing him in the kitchen

junk drawer. I want him to be up there in the china cabinet where everyone can see him.

By the end of the school year, Larry had been elected president of the school's sixth grade. He was involved in peer-conflict mediation and was earning A's and B's in every subject. He was among the academic leaders of Lewis's class.

While Larry represented a special example of accomplishment, the classroom was a special place for all the children, including the nine non-African Americans. (They were Latino, Pacific Islander, and Vietnamese.) The work was challenging and exciting. The students were presumed to have some level of literacy, which formed the foundation for increased competency. Reading, writing, and speaking were community activities that Lewis believed all students could participate in—and they did.

Julia Devereaux: "Gimme That Old-Time [Religion] Teaching"

If one were to design a "controlled study" Devereaux and Lewis would be closely matched on more variables than any other two teachers in my study. The two women are the same age and both have lived in the school community most of their lives. They attended the same state university (at different times) and were elementary, junior high, and senior high school classmates. In 1988 Devereaux succeeded Lewis as president of the teachers' association. Although weary of both the internal and external politics of the association, Lewis agreed to assist Devereaux in her first term as president.

The two obvious differences between the two that are important in this study are that Devereaux is African American whereas Lewis is white and that Devereaux believes in direct reading instruction, particularly using a basal text, whereas Lewis is committed to a whole-language approach to literacy.

Devereaux teaches at a school in the district that has made a commitment to training the teachers in a method espoused by a well-known African American educator in Chicago who established her own school for inner-city students. It is a no-frills, no-nonsense approach to teaching and learning. This basic-skills approach emphasizes phonics as the appropriate way to teach reading. "Classic" books in the European and African American tradition are a part of the curriculum. Devereaux transferred voluntarily to this school because of its philosophy; she was one of eight teachers the school sent to Chicago to receive training in this pedagogical approach.

Devereaux's family has always been a mainstay of the community. Her parents worked hard to raise a family there. Her father brought the family to California from Louisiana in the 1950s. He began work as a night custodian at a retail store and later became a bail bondsman. Her mother began as a window dresser at another retail store and went on to become assistant manager. Eventually her father opened a grocery store where both parents worked. Later, he studied for and earned his real-estate license and today is a well-respected realtor in the community.

Devereaux's family is active in the local Catholic church. Devereaux herself leads a Girl Scout troop. But her family is also known for a series of tragedies it has suffered. Both Devereaux and her sister were victims of violent crimes. Both have worked hard to put the trauma of the assaults behind them.

During the three years of my study, Devereaux taught fourth grade; however, she has taught every grade from second to eighth. Her classroom is a beehive. Students always seem to be all over the place, except when it is "reading time." Devereaux convenes the class for reading at 9:00 A.M. During the first twenty to thirty minutes of the day, the students may be involved in a variety of activities, including games, journal writing, handwriting, and spelling assignments, while Devereaux ties up loose ends, collecting monies for various projects or field trips, ordering books and materials, checking papers, or visiting with students. But at 9 o'clock all this activity comes to a halt.

Each of the twenty-five students in Devereaux's class this semester pulls out a basal reader and places it on top of the desk. Twenty-one of the twenty-five are African American, four are Latino. There are fifteen girls and ten boys.

Devereaux's reading lessons seem almost scripted. She begins with a phonics drill. A student goes to the front of the room, takes the pointer, and begins the drill by pointing to the chart above the chalkboard. The student points to the letter b: "Beating drum, beating drum, ba, ba, ba," she says. The class repeats in unison. She continues, "B sounds, 'bound.' What does 'bound' mean?" One student raises his hand and says, "Bound means to leap." The drill leader continues the drill through the consonants. Although this is a fourth-grade class, the words and terms they are asked to define seem sophisticated; they include "justice," "kinsman," "fatigue," "depositor," "lay waste," "preserve," "reunion," and "veranda." There is a high degree of participation in the drill. The drill leader calls on many different students.

At the conclusion of the drill, Devereaux thanks her and moves to the front of the room. She asks students to recap the last story they read. Depending on which skills were emphasized in the lesson and whether the students mastered those skills, she reviews some skills at the end of the story review.

One morning, Devereaux introduces the lesson by saying, "Today we're going to be reading about the first woman jockey." She directs the students' attention to a word list on the board. The following words are there: "influence," "atmosphere," "outlet," "developing," "demonstrate," "concentrate," and "equestrian." The students first attempt to define the words in words of their own and then use their glossaries. As they pronounce the words, Devereaux reminds them to sound them out phonetically.

She then begins calling on the students in round-robin fashion to read the story aloud. They seem eager to get a turn. She tries to divide the reading selection up so that everyone gets a turn. "Who haven't I heard from today?" she asks. Two hands go up. She calls on these students next. The entire class reads the last two paragraphs aloud in unison. Throughout the reading she asks a variety of recall questions. The entire experience seems rather ordinary, even boring.

I am anxious to talk to her about what she's doing.

I know it seems old-fashioned but I believe the students benefit from the structure. It's as if it were important for them to know what comes next. I have children in here who other teachers told me could not read. Heck, *they* told me they couldn't read. But I look them squarely in the eye in the beginning of the school year and tell them, you *will* read, and you will read *soon*. I tell my entire class we all have to know how to read and it's everybody's responsibility to make sure that everyone learns to read well. I pair up the better readers with the poorer ones and tell them that *the pair* gets a reading grade. They are allowed to do any number of things to help each other read. Although the school doesn't want us to do it I let them take their readers home. I also use some of those old, out-of-date basals as at-home readers for them. All students have a reading log in which they list what they read aloud to their parents the night before. The parents sign the logs. I award prizes for completing the reading logs. You may have noticed how quiet things got when the reading lesson began. I'm pretty easygoing about a lot of things, but I keep my reading time sacred.

Devereaux does a number of things to encourage reading. She has her own Book of the Month Club. Each month, Devereaux announces a book to read. Up to ten students may sign up to read it. She often purchases the books with her own money. The book club meets to talk about the book on their own time—at lunch with the teacher, in early-morning hours before school, or after school. No grades are given for participation in the club. Its reward is intrinsic.

The proof of Devereaux's pudding is indeed in the tasting. She suggested that I select her most difficult student, Michael, look at his cumulative file, and then listen to him read. Michael's file was two inches thick. He had been in a series of foster homes. His natural mother was a drug addict and had neglected him. Every teacher from first grade on had recommended that he be placed in a special day class. Everyone agreed he could not learn to read; he lacked the requisite skills and needed remedial attention that no one had the time to give him.

I asked Michael if he was willing to read something to me. His face lit up. He selected a book entitled *The Trouble with Tuck* from the shelf. It was a story about a girl and her dog. Although his reading was halting, Michael employed phonics skills and decoded the words that were not familiar. I asked him how long he had been such a good reader. "Only since I been in Miz Devereaux's class."

"Why is that?" I asked.

"I don't know, she just told me that I could read if I wanted to and she was going to help me want to. She said you can't stay in her class if you don't read. I want to stay."

Michael's reading partner was Jabari. Devereaux selected him because she knew that Jabari was very competitive and would personally take on the challenge of helping Michael to read. She supplied the pair with a variety of high-interest books about sports and athletes, rap stars, Hollywood actors. Devereaux often found reading tasks for Michael, such as reading the daily bulletin, food labels, baseball cards, cookbook directions, the telephone directory, maps; she tried to help him see the purpose of literacy. Michael also learned to take advantage of Devereaux's passion for reading. He was quick to ask her if he could read instead of doing some other task and she usually permitted him to do so. After all, here was a kid that everyone said would never read.

In third grade I was selected to go to the Reading Teacher. As I described earlier, the Reading Teacher was the person who worked with the accelerated group. As members of the special reading group we became a part of a special reading incentive program. We were rewarded for the number of books we read. To prove that we had actually read the books we said we had, we had to sign up for a "booktalk" with a teacher who had read the book. We scheduled these book talks during early mornings before school, at recess or lunchtime, or after school. It was exciting to sit down with an adult and talk about what we had read. We received certificates for reading twenty-five, fifty, or seventy-five books. If we read a hundred books we received a certificate and a pin. I did not rest until I got my certificate and pin. I reached that lofty plateau by the middle of fourth grade.

Lewis Versus Devereaux

On the surface Ann Lewis and Julia Devereaux employ very different strategies to teach reading. In some ways their differences represent the larger debate about literacy teaching, that of whole-language versus basal-text techniques. However, beneath the surface, at the personal ideological level, the differences between these instructional strategies lose meaning. Both teachers want their students to become literate. Both believe that their students are capable of high levels of literacy.

More specifically, several overarching tenets may be culled from both teachers' literacy programs. In sum, these tenets include the following:[5]

1. Students whose educational, economic, social, political, and cultural futures are most tenuous are helped to become intellectual leaders in the classroom. Both teachers direct a lot of their pedagogy toward African American boys. In Lewis's and Devereaux's classrooms it is "cool" or "def" to choose academic excellence. The teachers make the students' culture a point of affirmation and celebration. This means that they have to work actively against the constant and repeated denigration of Africa, Africans, and African Americans. By disrupting the notion of African American males as social outcasts, the teachers provide academic support for these boys and at the same time give the other students a new view of their fellow students.

2. Students are apprenticed in a learning community rather than taught in an isolated and unrelated way. The mention of this tenet here is a restatement of the idea that is presented in Chapters Four and Five. Both teachers treat their students as if they already know something. Rather than teach skills in an isolated, disconnected way, the two embed reading instruction within larger contexts. Even in Devereaux's more structured approach, the teaching of skills is contextualized.

3. Students' real-life experiences are legitimized as they become part of the "official" curriculum. Even though both of these teachers select literature for their students, they depend heavily on the experiences of their students to make the literature come alive. They are not writing on blank slates; instead, they are challenging conventional scripts by importing the culture and everyday experiences of the students into the literacy learning.

4. Teachers and students participate in a broad conception of literacy that incorporates both literature and oratory. What counts as literarily worthy is broadly defined in both classrooms. The students are allowed to ask their own questions and search for their own answers. By building on the students' knowledge, Lewis and Devereaux are able to teach complex ideas and skills without worrying that they are teaching above the students' reading level. Using multiple teaching strategies ensures that every child develops his or her reading ability without being ridiculed or embarrassed.

5. Teachers and students engage in a collective struggle against the status quo. Both teachers help their students understand that societal expectations for them are generally low. However, they support them by demonstrating that their own expectations are exceptionally high. Thus they indicate that to prove the prevailing beliefs wrong, teacher and students must join together.

6. Teachers are cognizant of themselves as political beings. In the case of both Lewis and Devereaux, the political nature of their work is manifested in their teacher association activities. Both have developed a sociopolitical and cultural vision that entails knowing that they need to move away from cultural-deficit explanations for African American students' low achievement levels and toward models of cultural excellence. They talk often with their students about the political nature of their work. The students are reminded that their progress toward cultural excellence is the mightiest weapon they possess to fight against a mediocre status quo.

Math in a Culturally Relevant Classroom

As we saw in Chapter Three, Margaret Rossi is an Italian American woman in her midforties. She began her teaching career in the late 1960s, when she was a Dominican nun. She has taught in both private and public schools and in both wealthy white communities and low-income communities of color. When this study was being done, she was teaching sixth grade. She was identified by a group of African American parents as a very effective teacher. In an ethnographic interview Rossi revealed that she knew that her students characterized her as "strict," but that she believed they respected her for being a demanding yet caring teacher.[6]

One morning, before an observation session, I met Rossi in the courtyard outside of her classroom. Although we exchanged pleasantries it was apparent that her mind was on the lesson she intended to teach. Earlier, she had talked to her students about the African origins of algebra; they had learned that the first definitive evidence of the use of algebra had appeared in the writings of

Ahmes, an Egyptian mathematician who lived around 1700 B.C. or earlier. They learned that, much later, the Greeks had contributed to the early development of algebra. Rossi felt that the "setting of the context" was important for motivating her students to learn algebra. She attempted to make them see that it had clear relations to their own heritage. There was no reason for them to think of it as "foreign." As she said to me, tongue-in-cheek, "It's not Greek to them!"

Rossi gave her room key to one of her students and asked her to go in and take care of some housekeeping chores. When the bell rang the students filed noisily in. They settled down after they entered the room and took their seats. At 8:35 Rossi greeted them with a cheery "good morning" and the students responded in kind. What followed the good morning greeting was a whirlwind of activity, perhaps too complex to explain fully here. However, I will attempt to summarize what transpired.

The entire time I observed her class that morning, Rossi and her students studied mathematics. Although they were engaged in problem solving through algebraic functions, no worksheets were handed out, no problem sets were assigned. The students, and Rossi, posed the problems.

Observing from a pedagogical standpoint, I saw Rossi make a point of getting every student involved in the lesson. She continually assured them that they were capable of mastering the problems. They cheered each other on and celebrated when they were able to explain how they arrived at their solutions. Rossi's time and energy were completely devoted to mathematics. Taking attendance, collecting lunch money, and all other tasks were handled by students in an unobtrusive, almost matter-of-fact manner that did not interfere with the mathematics discussion.

Rossi moved around the classroom as students posed questions and suggested solutions. She often asked, "How do you know?" to push the students' thinking. When students asked questions, Margaret was quick to say, "Who knows. Who can help him out here?" By recycling the questions (and consequently, the knowledge) Margaret helped her students understand that they were knowledgeable and capable of answering their own questions and those of others. However, Rossi did not shrink from her own responsibility as a teacher. From time to time she worked individually with students who seemed puzzled or confused. By asking a series of probing questions, she was able to help students organize their thinking about a problem and develop their own problem-solving strategies. The busy hum of activity in her classroom was directed toward mathematics. Every so often, she would suggest a problem and the students would work frantically to solve it. Each time she did this, a new set of questions and possible solutions came up. I was amazed at how comfortable the students seemed as the discussion proceeded. No one student or group of students dominated the session. Responses and questions came from all over the classroom.

As I sat taking notes, I heard a student exclaim, "This is easy!" Others nodded their heads in agreement. Never missing an opportunity to make mathematics accessible to her students, Rossi used such expressions to make a comment that reminded them how intelligent and capable they were.

At one point that morning, Rossi directed the students' attention to a page in the pre-algebra textbook she had scrounged up for the class. Rather than assign pages in the text, she showed the students how the textbook representation of what they had been doing appeared different. "Don't let it scare you," she urged. "You know how to solve problems like these." Rossi was thus assuring them that the good work they were doing in her class would carry through to district and state assessments; she knew that her students would be required to perform on standardized tests and that their performance might prove to be a significant factor in their mathematics placement the following year when they went on to middle school.

On another level Rossi may also have been reassuring her students that what they were doing was "legitimate." Because so much of this work was not out of a textbook, students (and perhaps their parents) may have wondered if they were doing "real" algebra.

By 9:59 it was time to prepare for recess. For almost an hour and a half Rossi and her students had been occupied with mathematical problem solving. She never once needed to stop to discipline or reprimand a student. The few instances in which students seemed to be off-task were quickly remedied when Rossi or another student posed a problem that brought their attention back to the discussion. Rossi told the students how proud she was of the way they had worked. She also told them that they were doing work that some eighth graders couldn't do. At 10 A.M., twenty-six happy sixth graders marched out to recess. Rossi smiled but she had a look of sadness in her eyes. She turned to me after the last student had left the room:

> They're so smart but so few teachers recognize it. I'm so afraid they will meet the same fate as last year's class. We work so hard to get them into algebra and then they go to the middle school where they're treated like they don't know anything. Last year's students were so bored with the math they had—it was actually arithmetic—that they started cutting math class to come back over here for me to teach them. When I explained that I couldn't teach them they just stopped going to math class altogether and failed for nonattendance.

Telling Isn't Teaching

I have described the classrooms of Ann Lewis, Julia Devereaux, and Margaret Rossi as examples of best practices. In this section, I describe a lesson carried out by Alex Walsh, one of my own student teachers.

Walsh was a twenty-two-year-old white student enrolled in a prestigious teacher preparation program. His student teaching assignment was in an upper-middle-class, predominately white community known for its excellent public school system. Alex was looking forward to the experience. He had been assigned to a sixth-grade class. His cooperating teacher was active on many district committees and had requested a student teacher who was comfortable taking the initiative and working independently. The class would probably have been characterized as an open classroom. Students worked at their own pace and in cooperative groups. One student who had cerebral palsy was mainstreamed into the class; a full-time teacher's aide worked with her. There were no African American students in the class but it was a culturally diverse class. The students represented several language groups—Spanish, Japanese, Chinese, Arabic—but all were fluent in English. Many of the students came from professional homes— the homes of doctors, attorneys, accountants, college professors.

It was my unofficial policy not to visit my student teachers on the same day that I visited the teachers participating in my study. It would be too easy to make unfair comparisons between the experts and the novices. However, on one particular day visiting both could not be avoided. After observing Margaret Rossi, I headed across the freeway to visit Alex Walsh.

Although the physical distance between the two schools was less than five miles, in resources—personnel, material, and students—they were worlds apart. Walsh's school was in a district that performed at the ninety-fifth percentile on standardized tests while the teachers in my study were working in a district that performed below the tenth percentile.

When I arrived in Walsh's classroom, the students were working on mathematics. The cooperating teacher was working with a group of twelve or thirteen students. Six or seven other students were working independently at their desks, and Walsh was working at a table in the back of the room with four boys—two white, two Latino. As I settled into a chair near Walsh's group I could hear him trying to explain how to change an improper fraction into a mixed number.

None of the students seemed to be paying attention to him. Two of the boys were poking each other with pencils; another was listening to his Walkman (although he denied it when questioned about why he had his hat pulled down over his ears). The fourth boy was staring out the window. After Walsh finished his explanation, he called on one of the pencil-pokers to solve a problem. The boy seemed to have no idea what to do. When asked if anyone could help, none of the others responded. Walsh gave his explanation another try.

This time he stopped many times to reprimand the boys for playing, giggling, and not paying attention. At the end of his explanation, he gave the boys three problems to solve. None of them was able to solve the problems. "This stuff is stupid!" remarked one boy. "I'm not doin' this," said another as he pushed his paper and pencil toward the center of the table. The other boys laughed. Walsh said "Okay, let's try doing the first one together." He began explaining the steps needed to change the improper fraction. The boys were not following. Walsh's patience wore thin. "Look!" he shouted. "I'm trying to teach you guys how to do this and you're not even paying attention."

Unsuccessfully, the boys tried to stifle a giggle. That was the last straw. Walsh sternly ordered them back to their seats and assigned them a page from their texts. The boys grumbled that they did not know how to do the problems, but Walsh ignored their complaints and told them he expected to see the problems before the math session was over. He glanced up at me. His face was red, perhaps from anger, perhaps from embarrassment—or both.

During our postobservation conference, I began by asking, "Tell me what you taught today." Walsh started telling me what he had intended and referred me to his lesson plan. "Yes," I commented, "You seem to have had a plan that fit your intent, but what did you teach?" Once again, he began to explain his intentions. He told me about how he had thought out the plan and how the boys had subverted it. "I could see that, Alex," I remarked. "But what did you *teach?*" He looked at me dejectedly and sighed.

"I guess I didn't teach anything," he said. I nodded in agreement. "Right, now we can talk about what went wrong."

Clearly, it is not fair to compare Alex Walsh's abilities with Margaret Rossi's. Rossi's seventeen years of experience *should* make her more skilled at teaching than Walsh. She has had the opportunity to make mistakes and grow as a teacher. And I am sure she has also had times when she "didn't teach anything." However, juxtaposing the two sessions illustrates just how different experts are from novices. If Walsh could have observed any of the teachers in my study, perhaps he might have learned some of the following:[7]

1. **When students are treated as competent they are likely to demonstrate competence.** Culturally relevant teaching methods do not suggest to students that they are incapable of learning. These teachers provide intellectual challenges by teaching to the highest standards and not to the lowest common denominator.

In Lewis's class, the students were expected to do more than read for literal meaning. Their responses to what they read were even more important than parroting back what the author had written. As they read books, Lewis asked what they thought the text meant and what connections they could make between the text and their own lives. Although Devereaux's reading class was more structured, the intellectual challenge was still there. Devereaux expected all students to become literate and she provided a variety of vehicles through which the students could develop their literacy. Rossi's decision to use challenging mathematics to motivate and teach her students proved to be an excellent way to improve both their mathematical skills and their conceptual skills. Doing algebra allowed them to build upon their competence and develop the confidence to meet even higher intellectual challenges.

2. **When teachers provide instructional "scaffolding," students can move from what they know to what they need to know.** In the classes of all three teachers, students are allowed

(and encouraged) to build upon their own experiences, knowledge, and skills to move into more difficult knowledge and skills. Rather than chastise them for what they do not know, these teachers find ways to use the knowledge and skills the students bring to the classroom as a foundation for learning.

3. The focus of the classroom must be instructional. Although a classroom is a complex and dynamic place, the primary enterprise must be to teach. In culturally relevant classrooms, instruction is foremost. Even when Lewis was reprimanding the students, she was instructing (explaining different parts of the brain). Devereaux's insistence on a sacrosanct reading period is her way of letting the students know that the time cannot be violated, not even by her personal relationship with them. Rossi's fast-paced, challenging mathematics leaves no room for off-task, noninstructional behavior. The message that the classroom is a place where teachers and students engage in serious work is communicated clearly to everyone.

Walsh's students did not take him seriously. Perhaps his inability to be effective with them came in part from his status as a student teacher; however, I have seen student teachers who are capable of managing a class. Walsh's group of students set their sights on disrupting his lesson; they were learning not to learn. Walsh's decisions to send them back to their seats with assignments they could not do (such as changing improper fractions to mixed numbers) taught them that instruction was not that important and that it could be used as a form of punishment.

4. Real education is about extending students' thinking and abilities. At no point in my student teacher's lesson did he assess what his students already knew. By building on some success—starting with something they had already mastered—he may have been more successful in engaging the students in the skills he intended to teach. As it was, his students decided that what he was talking about had nothing to do with them and he was unable to make the necessary connections. In contrast, Lewis, Devereaux,

and Rossi move their students to newer learning after establishing what they know and are able to do. Rather than a "drill-and-kill" approach to knowledge acquisition, their approach makes student learning a more contextualized, meaningful experience.

5. Effective teaching involves in-depth knowledge of both the students and the subject matter. The limited nature of the student teaching experience made Walsh's ability to build the necessary relationships between himself and his students difficult. If they knew more about one another, the children would have developed a greater commitment to learning because of their commitment to their teacher.

Lewis, Devereaux, and Rossi know their students well. They know which ones respond to subtle prodding and which ones need a more forceful approach. For them, good teaching starts with building good relationships. Rossi knew that one of her students was considered a candidate for special education. However, she believed that it was important to include him as a part of the class and hold him responsible for meeting high standards. To ensure that these expectations did not frustrate him, she spent more time with him, guaranteeing incremental success. Devereaux knew that Michael had a troubled home life. She knew that his poor reading ability was tied to the problems he confronted at home. So she worked to fill his school day with literacy experiences. By calling on him to read—directions, daily messages, and recreational materials—she cemented her relationship with him while he built his knowledge base and skills.

This chapter provided three examples of culturally relevant teaching in the basic skill areas of reading and math. Although each teacher has her own distinctive style, all share some essential qualities that were absent from the student teacher's practices. Despite his seemingly more desirable school environment, which resembled his own background, his effectiveness was compromised by the combination of his inexperience and his more assimilationist teaching orientation. Like many novices, the student teacher struggled with organizing students for instruction, but he also struggled with what he considered teaching to be. In his mind, teaching was the same as telling, and he did not question the hierarchical relationship he was attempting to establish between himself and the students. He assumed that the relationship between the students and himself was a one-way relationship: He would instruct; they would learn. He failed to treat them as if they knew anything and showed little enthusiasm for the material. He could not situate the lesson in the students' experience. For all of his efforts, his attempts to teach the students were futile. He gave up in frustration, believing the students had relinquished their privilege of being taught.

In the next and final chapter I consider what may lie ahead for culturally relevant teaching. I examine ways in which it may become a part of education classes and help all teachers, regardless of their race or ethnicity, to become more effective teachers of African American students.

* 7 *

Making Dreams into Reality

. . . arriving on a nightmare, praying for a dream . . .
—MAYA ANGELOU,
PRESIDENTIAL INAUGURATION
JANUARY 20, 1993

Throughout this book I have reported observations and conversations while interpreting and analyzing culturally relevant teaching practices. At the same time, I have interwoven a portion of my own story, for it is impossible to understand the stories of others in a vacuum. The practices I observed in these classrooms made sense to me because of my own experiences as an African American student. In this chapter I will address two separate but related ideas, the classroom teacher's personal responsibility and power and my vision of a culturally relevant school.

The Classroom Teacher's Power and Responsibility

The time I spent in the classrooms and with the teachers I studied was enjoyable, inspiring, and affirming: I was assured that there are some good teachers out there who can help African American students choose academic excellence and yet not compromise their cultural identities. But what does this mean? Of what use is it to know that a few teachers can do outstanding jobs with the very students that others believe incapable of being taught? Jonathan Kozol raises just this question in a discussion about a teacher named Corla Hawkins:

There are wonderful teachers such as Corla Hawkins almost everywhere in urban schools, and sometimes a number of such teachers in a single school. It is tempting to focus on these teachers, and, by doing this, to paint a hopeful portrait of the good things that go on under adverse conditions. There is, indeed a growing body of such writings, because they are consoling.

The rationale behind much of this writing is that pedagogic problems in our cities are not chiefly matters of injustice, inequality, or segregation, but of insufficient information about teaching strategies. If we could simply learn "what works" in Corla Hawkins's room, we'd then be in a position to repeat this all over Chicago and in every other system.[1]

Kozol's point is that it is easy to look at the exceptions in order to dismiss the rule. For this reason, what I have tried to express in these pages is not a cult of personality.

Rather, I have tried to stress the principles at work. Culturally relevant teaching is about questioning (and preparing students to question) the structural inequality, the racism, and the injustice that exist in society. The teachers I studied work in opposition to the system that employs them. They are critical of the way that the school system treats employees, students, parents, and activists in the community. However, they cannot let their critique reside solely in words. They must turn it into action by challenging the system. What they do is both their lives and their livelihoods. In their classrooms, they practice a subversive pedagogy. Even in the face of the most mundane curricular decisions these teachers make a stand:

Last year we had to use a book that the district required. I had a lot of problems with that book so I went to the publisher of another company and got him to give me another set of books. I'm using what my kids need.

—JULIA DEVEREAUX

I'm not a textbook teacher. I use the texts as resources but I have to teach what the children need, not what the district wants. The students' needs come first.

—Peggy Valentine

I have problems with the administration. Many times they have less experience than I have and I feel I could tell them a few things. I refuse to set my philosophy aside for one that doesn't have the best interests of the children and the community at heart.

—Elizabeth Harris

Very quietly, I do what I want. (A laugh.) I do! But I don't make a big deal about it. I don't. I mean, if the administrators and I were sitting here talking about it I would tell them what I think, but I generally don't make a big point about bucking the system. I just do it because the kids are worth it.

—Margaret Rossi

I finally told my principal this year that I did not use the mandated texts and she didn't say anything because she knew the kind of results I was getting and she knew the kind of results my colleagues were getting. I'm responsible for this classroom. I've worked long enough to know what will work and what doesn't work. I'm not going to just blatantly tell a principal what I'm not going to do. I'm just going to do what I need to do in order for my students to achieve.

—Pauline Dupree

I guess because I have such a strong personality many administrators have left me alone. After forty years of teaching, I know how to get the parents of the community to support what I'm doing because they understand my level of commitment. The students and their needs must come first. I'm not here to make a principal, a superintendent, or for that matter, myself, look good. I have work to do and people can either get on board to help me do it or stay out of my way.

—GERTRUDE WINSTON

Thus even though Kozol also has a point when he cites the need for systemic change, this does not give teachers license not to struggle against the oppressive and inequitable institutions in which they work. In many ways, the teachers' struggle is similar to what legal scholar Derrick Bell calls the struggle against the *permanence of racism*: "Not that we legitimate the racism of the oppressor. On the contrary, we can only delegitimate it if we can accurately pinpoint it. And racism lies at the center, not at the periphery; in the permanent, not in the fleeting; in the real lives of black and white people, not in the sentimental caverns of the mind."[2]

Extending Bell's concept to education, we must not legitimate the inequity that exists in the nation's schools, but attempt to delegitimate it by placing it under scrutiny. In the classrooms, working in opposition to the system is the most likely road to success for students who have been discounted and disregarded by the system. But how do we cultivate this kind of oppositional nature in our teachers?

Motivating Teachers; Changing Teaching Practices

Lipman's research in restructured schools suggests that despite the movement toward more localized and democratic administrations and greater material and personnel support, teachers' ideologies about the likely academic success of African American students remains unchanged: Deep down they do not believe that African American students can be successful academically.[3]

Grant and Secada reviewed the literature on multicultural teacher education and found a lack of empirical studies in this area. They found no studies that address the ideological blinders that prospective teachers may have developed as a result of their own cultural and educational experiences.[4] Ahlquist argues that attempts to get at these deep ideologies engender resistance. Prospective teachers do not easily relinquish beliefs and attitudes about themselves or others. Thus a serious effort toward preparing teachers to teach in a culturally relevant manner requires a rethinking of the teacher preparation process.[5] Some ideas to help foster the kind of attitude needed were expressed by the teachers in my study.

1. Recruit teacher candidates who have expressed an interest and a desire to work with African American students. Most teacher candidates are young, white, and female and would prefer to work with students with backgrounds similar to their own.[6] Further, even if we were to convince all of the current minority collegians to become teachers, we would still have a shortage of minority teachers.[7] Thus the pool from which we select must necessarily include whites. Still, we must encourage those who really want to teach African American students. We must also look for more innovative and nontraditional ways to bring the right people into teaching. Schools and universities must provide access and resources for committed people to get the education and credentials they need in programs like the one Ann Lewis attended. To determine the commitment of these prospective teachers, a condition of their admittance to such programs would be working in a predominately African American school for a specified period of time.

2. Provide educational experiences that help teachers understand the central role of culture. Despite the current trend toward multicultural education, prospective teachers typically go through workshops and courses that focus only superficially on material culture. Thus they come away with a "foods-and-festivals" approach to individual cultures; they learn to make a pinata or sing a spiritual. A more sophisticated preparation program may require them to take a content-rich course on one or more ethnic groups but even here they get little idea of the ways in which the course relates to elementary school children. And rarely do they have the opportunity to examine the central aspects of their own or the predominate American culture: Often they believe that "culture is what other people have; what we have is just *truth*." Because these teachers' own cultural backgrounds remain unexamined, they have no way to challenge their intrinsic assumptions. For example, here is a statement from one of the participants in a staff development session I conducted:

> Parents can also be roadblocks to their child's education. They move a lot, they lack interest in the child's education, they don't help with homework or supplies, they don't come to conferences. What can I do? I don't have time to work on these issues with parents.

This teacher was expressing the frustrations of many teachers. She felt overwhelmed and powerless in the face of the problems that the students were confronting and, consequently, that she was confronting. But if we deconstruct her statement, we will reveal some powerful assumptions about both schooling and her role as a teacher.

First, this teacher describes her students' parents as roadblocks. Thus she seems to assume that her teaching of the students is predicated on the assistance of the parents. Further, the kinds of things she lists as parental "roadblocks" actually may be beyond the parents' control. Do the parents move a lot because they wish to or because they need to move to get work or better living circumstances? Is their lack of interest deliberate or do the parents lack knowledge about how to express interest in ways that the school recognizes? Perhaps they believe that merely sending a child to school is a strong demonstration of concern for education. Not providing supplies may be an indication of a lack of financial resources; the parents cannot give what they do not have. Not coming to conferences may merely indicate that the school is across town and that their children are bused to it; perhaps the parents lack adequate transportation. Further, perhaps the parents have not learned that "going to school" means attendance at times other than when their children have been reprimanded.

Second, this teacher views the parents' behavior in relation to her own experiences as a student, parent, and teacher. For years this school that she works in served a white, upper-middle-class community where parents not only participated in the school but also determined how it functioned—who was hired and fired, what the curriculum should be, how monies were allocated. But now, with the institution of busing to achieve desegregation, many of these parents deserted the school and sent their children to private schools, while the new students, low-income, African American children, have parents who view the school with suspicion and hostility. And even those who have favorable (or even indifferent) attitudes toward the school lack the time and resources to get as involved with it as their predecessors did. When life is a struggle on a daily basis, going to school—particularly a school located across town in a white community—is one of these parents' lowest priorities.

I raise these points not in an attempt to absolve parents of their responsibility toward their children's education but to encourage teachers to look more broadly and carefully at the causes of the behaviors they see, to develop multiple perspectives, and to make a commitment to working with their students, regardless of parental participation (or lack thereof). Culturally relevant teaching preparation would raise these kinds of questions about the assumptions about students, parents, and communities the teachers bring with them.

3. Provide teacher candidates with opportunities to critique the system in ways that will help them choose a role as either agent of change or defender of the status quo. Several years ago I taught

an introduction to education class. I usually began the semester
with the question, "Why do we have schools?" The students who
enrolled in this course were usually sophomores and juniors
who expected to go on to a career in teaching. Overwhelmingly,
their response was, "So that we can be prepared to work."

So prevalent is the message that education equals work that
prospective teachers focus primarily on this aspect of it. When I
presented the students with information about how a recessionary
economy affects everyone, even teachers, they were at a loss as to
how to justify this vocational purpose. More confounding still were
the data I presented on how racism and sexism affect an individual's opportunity to work regardless of educational qualifications.

Thus we had to begin to examine some of the most fundamental social purposes of education. Presenting the current educational method as a conservative one designed to maintain or
reproduce the status quo gave the students a unique challenge.
How could they knowingly participate in a system that put
children of color (and other groups) at a disadvantage while it
granted privileges to people like them? By examining some of the
underlying assumptions about education, they realized that education is not an apolitical enterprise. It serves a function in the
society and individual teachers can act consciously to support or
oppose those social functions or they can act unconsciously (and
mindlessly) in ways that *invariably* support them.

**4. Systematically require teacher candidates to have prolonged
immersion in African American culture.** Most teacher candidates
do not need an immersion experience in white middle-class culture
because they are either products of it or have been acculturated
and/or assimilated enough to negotiate it successfully. However,
when beginning teachers come into minority communities, many
are unable to understand the students' home language, social interaction patterns, histories, and cultures. Thus they cannot truly educate the students. Their perceptions of deficiency and competence
are socially and culturally constructed. Without greater exposure

to the students' culture teachers lack the tools with which to make sense of much that transpires in the classroom.

Further, they cannot serve effectively in a decontextualized manner. Immersion in the community to learn who the community leaders are, where the community centers are, which people command respect, what matters to the children in the community, all provide teachers with needed information about how to work *with* rather than *against* the community.

5. Provide opportunities for observation of culturally relevant teaching. "Master teacher" may be one of the most misunderstood and misused terms in teacher education. What most preparation programs really have are "cooperating teachers," who supervise the student teaching experience. The selection of these cooperating teachers can be haphazard. In some instances, student teachers are used as rewards for teachers who have found favor with the principal. Thus, in an attempt to lighten the favored individual's workload, for example, the principal may discount the needs of the student teacher or the expertise of another faculty member. Or the principal may place a student teacher with a teacher who simply needs help; the thinking here is that having anybody else in the classroom—no matter how inexperienced—will improve the situation. The student teacher becomes an unwitting witness or accomplice to bad practice, possibly helping the principal document the poor practices in order to remove the teacher. In still other instances the principal may merely ask, "Who would like to have a student teacher this year from the local university?" With no consideration given to expertise and experience, the assignment of student teachers becomes just another administrative task. It is important to note that such random, unthoughtful assignment of student teachers is not limited to principals. Teachers and university personnel are also responsible for some of this unhealthy professional behavior.

Often the best teachers want nothing to do with the patronage and bureaucracy involved in student teacher assignments.

But by providing real incentives (such as stipends, salary increments, fringe benefits), committed teachers can be induced to participate in truly mentoring those students who will one day take their places in schools in African American communities.

6. Conduct student teaching over a longer period of time and in a more controlled environment. Student teaching assignments may be as short as six weeks or as long as a year. Typically, they require at least a semester (twelve to twenty weeks). But no matter the length, education students routinely report that the clinical or student-teaching experience is the most valuable part of their preparation. But because they are so short, the current student teacher programs fail to give students adequate opportunity to get to know the students, the school, or the community to which they are assigned.

Because of the discontinuity between grade school and university calendars, student teachers may be placed in classrooms that are already up and running; thus they have no idea how they came to be the way they are. Further, the children in the classrooms have already developed allegiances and relationships with the cooperating teacher and may identify the student teacher as an interloper, no matter how benign.

With real apprenticeships—beginning before the start of the school year and lasting until the end—student teachers could see the evolution and development of the classroom over time. They could see the ups and downs that the teachers experience regardless of their expertise, and have the opportunity to make changes in their own practices. They would not be constrained to "get it right" according to the specifications of their supervisor within the space of six to eight weeks.

In addition to the length of time student teachers spend in classrooms, there is the problem of the nature of the environment. As mentioned previously, by coming in after the start of the school year, the student teacher may be an unwelcome addition to the classroom.

Ideally, the student teacher goes on to teach in his or her own classroom. However, even here some changes in the program would be useful. Rather than the sink-or-swim approach we provide for beginning teachers, where they are assigned a full class load from their first year of teaching, we need to give new teachers a chance to practice their craft in smaller classes. If we really care about issues like student achievement and new teacher retention, we must organize the school in more supportive ways. Organizing teaching teams might be a way to reduce the class load for new teachers without totally marginalizing them. For example, a teaching team of two teachers and forty to forty-five children might include two additional adults, a teacher's aide and a student teacher, for example. This four-member team would develop the curriculum and instructional strategies to be used in the classroom. The team would schedule preparation and observation times for each member. The four could design the kinds of professional development experiences that would meet the specific needs of the individual team members. Instead of having to attend workshops and lectures that the administrator deemed appropriate for the entire school, the team members could decide what they wanted and needed to learn and then could arrange for training in those areas. In such a program, the student teacher would have the opportunity to function fully as a teacher under the careful tutelage of three other team members and the mistakes that he or she would surely make would become opportunities for learning and improvement.

A Vision of a Culturally Relevant School

I began this book with a question: Do African American students need separate schools? I conclude with an answer: What African American students need are *better* schools. I contend that culturally relevant teaching practices would be an integral part of these schools. But how else would a school that best serves the needs of African American students and their community be constructed?

An often-asked question of people of color, women, and other marginalized groups is "What is it you people want?" Surprisingly for some, what these people want is not very different from what most Americans want: an opportunity to shape and share in the American dream. But when these people say what they want, it is seen as "separatism," "reverse racism" (a strange concept), "tribalism," and "special privilege."

Although I cannot presume to speak for the entire African American community, because it is not a monolithic group, I can try to express the hopes and desires of the African American parents I met during this study and the teachers who participated in it.

1. Provide educational self-determination. Although they didn't use the word self-determination both parents and teachers complained about local, state, and federal mandates that organize schools and curricula in ways that are not meaningful for their children. One parent spoke of a daughter who knew how to do cursive writing when she was seven years old but was told she had to print because, "We don't do cursive until third grade." Another added, "If we're behind in the class we're a problem and if we're ahead we're a problem. They seem to have some perfect student in their minds that our children can never be."

Many of the efforts aimed toward African American immersion schools, which I discussed in Chapter One, are a response to this call for self-determination. This desire is no different from what all parents want from the schools their children go to. Middle-class parents tell schools what they want and they expect the schools to respond positively to their demands.

I am reminded of a meeting between upper-middle-class white parents and a principal and a school board member to discuss the school's sports program. Both the principal and the board member insisted that there was no money in the budget to fund the kind of program the parents requested.

Suddenly, one man in the audience stood up; he looked as if he had just come from work—his suit jacket was draped over his arm, his necktie was loosened. He cleared his throat and said, "Let me get this straight. You're saying we can't have what we want for our kids." The board member replied, "It's not that we don't want to give you want you want, but there is no money." The parent straightened his shoulders, looked squarely at the board member, and said in a calm, even tone, "Now, you listen. These are our schools and we can have *whatever* we want. If you can't give it to us, we'll get rid of you and find somebody who can."

Whether he was just blowing off steam or not did not matter to me. I was taken aback by the sheer personal power he exhibited. He had a clear understanding of self-determination and his access to it. And indeed, six months later the sports program was approved. The principal had died of a heart attack (I infer no causal relation here).

2. Honor and respect the students' home culture. Many critics interpret this to mean that African American educational advocates and parents want to supplant the entire curriculum with an "African" curriculum. However, what I see parents, teachers, and community activists advocating is merely an accurate and fair representation of African American culture in the school curriculum.

The typical experience in the schools is a denigration of African and African American culture. Indeed, there is a denial of its very existence. The language that students bring with them is seen to be deficient—a corruption of English. The familial organizations are considered pathological. And the historical, cultural, and scientific contributions of African Americans are ignored or rendered trivial.

In order to help teachers understand the wealth and strength of the African American culture, a colleague and I conduct workshops in which we ask teachers to imagine that African Americans are new arrivals in this country, like many other recent immigrants.

What kind of America do they find? While the question has no correct answer and calls upon teachers to use some historical imagination, it typically yields a long list of cultural contributions and a vision of a very different United States. For example, teachers have suggested that we would not have the rich musical heritage provided by blues, jazz, and gospel. Others have suggested that the moral conscience of the nation might not have been heightened without the experience of the civil rights movement. A number of teachers have suggested that the country would be unrecognizable because we might have failed to develop beyond the original thirteen colonies without the labor of enslaved African Americans who developed the economy of the South. Almost always, someone has suggested that some other group would be "on the bottom" of a society that insists on cultural ranking.

We often end these sessions by asking the teachers to keep the memory of these contributions in the forefront of their minds when they teach African American children. Thus they will remember that they are teaching children who are heirs to a great tradition of art, music, dance, science, invention, oratory, and so on.

3. Help African American students understand the world as it is and equip them to change it for the better. When my son was in first grade he was the only African American child in his class. His teacher, an African American woman, seemed particularly tough on him. As a young parent I was dismayed at what I saw as unfair treatment. In a parent-teacher conference she said to me, "I've seen too many black children, particularly boys, get messed over in this school. I'm being hard on him because he's got to be tough enough to endure." I didn't like what she said but I knew she was right. I could not shield my son from the realities of racism. He *did* need a school experience that made him better prepared than his white peers.

African American children cannot afford the luxury of shielding themselves with a sugar-coated vision of the world. When their parents or neighbors suffer personal humiliations and discrimination because of their race, parents, teachers, and neighbors need to explain why. But beyond those explanations, parents, teachers, and neighbors need to help arm African American children with the knowledge, skills, and attitude needed to struggle successfully against oppression. These, more than test scores, more than high grade-point averages, are the critical features of education for African Americans. If students are to be equipped to struggle against racism they need excellent skills from the basics of reading, writing, and math, to understanding history, thinking critically, solving problems, and making decisions; they must go beyond merely filling in test sheet bubbles with Number 2 pencils.

So what would a school that offered this kind of experience look like? One can only speculate, but having spent two years in eight classrooms that tried to make these kinds of experiences happen, I am willing to commit some speculations to paper.

Theodore Sizer had *Horace's School*.[8] Former Education Secretary William Bennett had James Madison High School.[9] Let me imagine what I will call Paul Robeson Elementary.

Paul Robeson Elementary School is located in a low-income, predominately African American community. More than merely a school, Robeson is a neighborhood center and gathering place that is open from 6:00 A.M. to 10:00 P.M. It includes a day care center, a preschool, a health clinic, and a job training center. Local civic and church groups use the school as a meeting place. If one needs information about the community, the school is the likely place to locate it.

The banner across the main hallway of the school reads, "It takes a whole village to educate a child." Robeson's teaching staff is multicultural. There are African American, Latino, Asian American, and white teachers. However, every credentialed adult at Robeson, not just the teachers, teaches a class—the principal, the counselor, the special teachers. This means that classes are relatively small—twelve to fifteen students. There are no "pull out" programs, such as those used by many federally funded programs that require students to be taken out of their regular classrooms to receive remedial instruction while simultaneously depriving them of the instruction that is occurring in the regular class. There is no separate "special day" class for students evaluated as learning-disabled. Instead, students with learning disabilities are integrated into the regular classrooms and receive additional attention with the help of teachers' aides, the classroom teacher, and more advanced peers.

Robeson has one requirement—that its students be successful. The curriculum is rigorous and exciting. The student learning is organized around problems and issues. For example, one fourth-grade class is studying how cities develop. The students have studied cities in ancient African kingdoms, Europe, and Asia. They are studying their own city. They have taken trips to City Hall and have seen the City Council in action. The mayor visited their classroom. In current events they read about the city news. Groups of students are working on solutions to problems specific to their city. The problems include the city's budget deficit, homelessness, the poor condition of roads, and crime—particularly drug-related crime.

The students have read Carl Sandberg's poetry about his beloved Chicago. They have studied architecture—buildings and bridges. They have studied geography and urban planning. They have written letters to the editor of a city newspaper about conditions in the city and in their neighborhood. Each student is an "expert" in some aspect of cities. Together they are planning an exhibition that will be shown in the evening so that their parents and other community members can attend.

All students at Robeson Elementary participate in a community service program. The students in the primary grades usually participate as a class group. Community service activities include visiting a local nursing home, where students participate in the Adopt-a-Grandparent program. They also participate in neighborhood cleanup days and recycling drives. The older students develop their own community service projects, which are approved by their teachers. They usually work in small groups or in pairs. Occasionally, intermediate class will take on a project such as becoming readers at the local library, volunteering in the pediatric ward of the hospital, and planting and maintaining a community garden.

Parents play an important role at Robeson. Each household is assessed twenty hours of volunteer service to the school. Some volunteer one hour a week in the classroom. Others participate in the school's Artists and Scholars in Residence program. Parents who participate in the local church choir offer their musical skills. Others share their cooking, sewing, knitting, woodworking, or athletic talents.

School governance at Robeson involves the principal, the teachers, the parents, and the students. The school council meets once a month to discuss the curriculum, instruction, personnel, and finances. The council members determine school policy and hiring and firing issues, and they constitute the school's disciplinary board.

One of Robeson's unique qualities is its residence program. By working with local social-service agencies Robeson obtained the use of a renovated small apartment building nearby to house students whose family lives are in turmoil. Under the best of circumstances students spend only a short time at the residence; in some unfortunate cases they spend the entire year there. By living in a center in their own community, they do not have to leave Robeson or the neighborhood they know. The residence is not for students with disciplinary problems. It is designed simply to alleviate family stresses.

As a testament to the success of Robeson Elementary School, its students score above the national norm on standardized tests, but Robeson does not make a fuss over its test score performance. The school community knows that in a caring, supportive environment where all of the children are made to feel special, test scores are but one of the marks of accomplishment that can be expected.

This fictional school, Paul Robeson Elementary School, has a basis in reality. In Cartwright's description of her tenure as principal of an inner-city Philadelphia school she described many of the features outlined in this vision of an effective educational environment for poor African American students. Her school provided many of the services that the students' homes could not provide and was not judgmental of either the students or their parents.[10] Further, each of the features described here are present in some form in some schools across this nation. By consolidating them into a complete package, I have attempted to develop a vision of a culturally relevant school.

The Robeson school is a place where the eight teachers I have presented in this book would find an ideological home. Their high expectations would be the norm. The notion of linking student learning with active citizenship through community service would be a schoolwide notion. Their understanding of the students' culture as a valuable and integral aspect of their teaching and the students' learning would be shared by the entire school community.

Indeed, my imaginings of Robeson Elementary School are not as far-fetched as one might believe. The commitment of the eight teachers with whom I worked gives me hope as a teacher educator who is committed to helping new teachers reflect carefully about what it means to teach toward personal empowerment and liberation. As I look back on my work with these dreamkeepers, I am mindful of the meaning that dreams have held for African Americans. From the spirituals of enslaved African Americans to the powerful oratory of civil rights leaders, African American dreams have challenged the "American Dream" to make itself manifest for those citizens who have been excluded from full citizenship. African Americans have believed that as long as they continued to dream, there was still a reason to look toward tomorrow. One of the most tangible vehicles for these dreams has been education—even when it was substandard and alienating. African Americans believed that somehow education could make their dreams a reality. I too believe and hope that if we can dream it, we can surely do it.

AFTERWORD

*

Your old men shall dream dreams,
Your young men shall see visions.

—JOEL 2:28

There was another way to honor all the teachers in the original study—that was to continue to find teachers and other school personnel who were using their work to improve their own practice. I thought of the first group of eight teachers as "existence proofs"—evidence that there were teachers capable of teaching African American students to high levels of achievement, even in the midst of a "teach to the test" culture that now dominates many of our schools.

The New Dreamkeepers

During my travels across the country I have encountered a number of incredible teachers who easily fall into the category of "dreamkeeper." They are teachers who focus on student learning, cultural competence, and sociopolitical consciousness in their work with African American and Latino students. Their work underscores the significance of the work of the original teachers I studied. They are not flukes or oddities. Such teachers exist throughout our country and we need to acknowledge and celebrate them. In this Afterword to the original book I present some brief summaries of their work and remind the readers that this work is enduring and likely to transcend a variety of educational reforms and trends.

Beverly Johannson

One of the classrooms I have visited over the years is of a woman who I will call Beverly Johannson. She was a white working-class woman who became a teacher after having been a single mother with meager financial resources. She studied comparative literature and later took advantage of a program that allowed her to earn teacher certification. She teaches second- and third-graders in a school serving low and moderate income families. At first glance it would be easy to dismiss her as one of those "1960s" era teachers. Her curriculum focuses on issues of social justice and her students learn about racism, sexism, and heterosexism. But she is not an ideologue. The students learn about these things in the context of building and improving skills in reading, writing, and mathematics. I was particularly struck by the respect she showed her students. Although they are seven- and eight-year-olds, she never talks down to them. She allows the students to call her by her first name but they say "Bev" with the utmost respect. Each week the students work on writing a class newsletter to let their parents and other community members know what they are studying. Bev regularly invites people from the community into her classroom—a geologist, a midwife (with a placenta)— and extends the classroom by having the students communicate with seven- and eight-year-olds in other countries. Beverly is also a scholar. In addition to her work in classrooms with students, Beverly has regularly written about her work and published it in journals whose primary audience is teachers. Bev has remained committed to the notions that children are thinkers and problem solvers and the role of the teacher is to pose important questions to and with them in spite of the increasing narrowing of the curriculum and the task of teaching only to a standardized test. Bev has resisted this narrow vision of teaching in the face of changing school administrators and colleagues.

Patti Brighton

I encountered another teacher in one of my graduate courses. Patti Brighton, a white, middle-class woman, was teaching English and drama at a local high school. As a drama teacher she struggled with the fact that many white, middle-class students and their families believed that the school's drama department was their sole purview. It was not that they wanted to be actors or have some other career in theater but, rather, they saw drama as a way to improve their resumes as they pursued selective colleges and universities. Determined to open the ranks of drama and theater to an increasingly diverse student body, Patti decided to stage a play by a well-known, award-winning African American playwright who wrote of the African American experience in the United States. The play had no non-white parts and its selection caused consternation among some white students and their parents. Patti justified her choice in two ways. First, she pointed out that she had told the students in the beginning of the school year that there would be two productions this year and they would act in one play and crew in the other. The play by the African American playwright would be the one that white members of the drama group would crew.

The second point was that the history of dramatic productions in the school over the past ten years indicated that the school had never produced a play by an African American playwright. No plays by Lorraine Hansberry, August Wilson, Amiri Baraka, or Douglas Turner Ward were ever showcased at the school. The list of plays were the usual suspects—"Oklahoma," "Bye-Bye Birdie,"

"Annie Get Your Gun," "Our Town," "Death of a Salesman," and Shakespearean comedies and tragedies.

Patti's understanding of the exclusion that so many African American students feel is linked to her own lived experience as an adoptive parent of an African American boy. She saw first-hand the way her son was marginalized and excluded from any number of academic and social opportunities and was determined not to participate in that kind of behavior. Patti joined her school's equity team and worked to confront racism. Like Beverly, Patti was also a scholar. She completed her doctoral degree by working on a dissertation that looked at her colleagues who joined in the effort to combat racism and what it took for them to challenge the resistance of those teachers who did not want to think about or talk about the way racism was compromising the educational opportunities of so many students.

Elizabeth Collins

A third classroom that comes to mind is that of a woman I will call Elizabeth. Like Patti, Elizabeth Collins, another white, middle-class teacher, also teaches theater and drama and she, too, was concerned that white middle-class students believed that they alone were entitled to star in every school production. Rather than stage a play about the lives of people of color, Elizabeth formed a new theater company whose primary purpose is to serve as an educational vehicle for informing the audience about racism, sexism, heterosexism, disability, and classism. Elizabeth insists that the theater group contain students from all ethnic groups represented in the school and the students write their own skits that reflect their daily experiences. On average Elizabeth's students perform fifty to sixty times before elementary and middle school audiences each school year. Her work has so excited the students that each year, African American and Latino students approach Elizabeth to learn what it will take in order for them to join the theater group in the coming year. Elizabeth uses the students' enthusiasm for the on-stage work as a springboard for delving into sociopolitical issues that regularly emerge in the school and in their daily lives.

Matt Crosley

A fourth teacher, a young white upper-middle-class man I will call Matt Crosley, has one of the more interesting stories I have encountered. Matt grew up in a beautiful, upper-middle-class community, where he attended an exclusive prep school. As a teenager he loved basketball and began volunteering in a predominately African American community where he coached basketball. He was impressed with how smart his charges were but puzzled by the fact that they seemed so disaffected with school. During his collegiate years Matt begged his way into some graduate course that focused on the education of African American children and wrote his senior thesis on the question of why black children could not get a good education in their own communities. Following his bachelor's degree Matt enrolled in and completed a teacher certification program. He taught in a local high school, where he saw many of the children he coached continuing to fail miserably. After a few years Matt dusted off his senior thesis and converted it into a business plan and marketed it to a number of corporate heads. His timing was excellent, as many of the companies were benefiting from an economic boom.

Matt and one of his high school colleagues opened a school in the middle of the African American community with eight students. Today the school serves 240 sixth- through twelfth-graders and has a 100 percent high school graduation rate and a 100 percent college-going rate. Even though Matt opened a private school, he restricted admittance to students living in the community. Matt has moved into a home located on the campus and is an active participant in community politics. Students at his school take only college preparatory courses and attend school from 8:00 A.M to 5:00 P.M. All students have at least one tutorial in the middle of the day for additional one-on-one help and all seniors participate in an independent research project in which they conduct a symposium before an audience of peers and experts. Matt says that the school is proof that what he believed about the students from those early days of coaching is true—they can learn, and learn at very high levels of achievement.

I once visited Matt's home (on campus) over a school holiday, and there were about seven students at school working on projects. The school only admits those students who want to attend (not just those whose parents want them to attend). Although the cost of education for each student is approximately $14,000 per year, all of the school's students are on full scholarship. The students must commit to attending every day and doing their homework. Matt and his teachers do not care if students come to them with knowledge and skill deficits. They believe it is their job to address those. Over the past half dozen years students at Matt's school have won the journalism award for a newspaper judged far superior to those of their white, upper-middle-class counterparts in the wealthier school communities that surround theirs.

Yvonne Jackson

The next dreamkeeper is an African American working-class woman who called me on the telephone to insist that I come and visit her school on the east coast of the United States. I will call her Yvonne Jackson. She is a first-time principal and has turned around an elementary school in a working-class section of a large city school district that is notoriously failing most students. When I was finally able to visit, I saw an entire elementary school that had rallied around the principles of culturally relevant teaching and pushed students to perform at exceptionally high levels.

In one classroom the kindergarten teacher had to leave to help one of her students, who was having some problems in the bathroom. She casually said, "Miss Annie, can you take over the class until I get back?" Miss Annie strolled to the front of the room and helped the children with the word wall, pretending every so often that she did not know a beginning sound while the children shouted with glee, "No, it doesn't go there!" Miss Annie was not a teacher or an instructional aide. Miss Annie was the janitor but like every adult I met in the school, she took responsibility for the children's learning.

In a classroom for students with severe disabilities I met a teacher with severe disabilities. On her braces she moved deftly around the classroom and permitted no excuses for students not completing their work. When one student who had recently returned from another of his many surgeries complained that he could not speak very loudly, the teacher told him that she would listen very carefully but it would not be an excuse for his not completing his work. "Don't you know that I decorated this entire room by myself? Don't you realize that I still go skiing? Don't you realize that I'm more interested in your ability than your disability?" Yvonne told me she pulled lots of strings to get this teacher and she was never sorry she did.

In a first grade classroom I met a teacher who had a student from rural Pakistan. The little girl had transferred from another school, where the teacher had insisted she suffered from a severe disability because she did not speak. Yvonne's first grade teacher said, "I could not assume that she had a disability. She came from the other side of the world and she did not know anyone. I assumed that she is overwhelmed by her new environment." The teacher told me that one weekend she was wandering through a half-priced bookstore and found a travel book on Pakistan. She purchased it and handed it to the little girl. In a few moments she was flipping the pages with eyes as wide as saucers. Finally, the little girl who had not spoken a word exclaimed, "Pakistan . . . I live Pakistan." Next she pointed to a picture and said, "Goat . . . I have goat!" The teacher told me, "I knew she was bright. I just had to find a way to reach her."

Every classroom I visited throughout the school revealed teachers who were serious about their students' abilities and they pointed to Yvonne's leadership as the catalyst. One teacher told me she had been teaching more than twenty years but she did not really feel like a professional until she worked with Yvonne. In addition to supporting the teachers and staff Yvonne reached out to the community. Each month her school had a games night. "It's supposed to be a games night, but really it's Bingo night," Yvonne remarked. "I personally hate Bingo but my families love it so one Friday a month we open the school late and invite in the community to play. It's a great time for parents to get to know their children's teachers and to let me know what's on their minds. We do whatever we can to work more closely with our students and their families."

Ashanti Morris

Ashanti Morris, a working-class African American woman, is an experienced mathematics teacher who has worked for many years in an independent school. I learned of her after she successfully passed the National Board for Professional Teaching Standards secondary mathematics certification. She contacted me by mail and said the following: "I have just earned National Board Certification in secondary mathematics but I have no idea if my students are actually learning. Would you be willing to look at my videotape and tell me what you think?"

I popped the videotape into the VCR and saw powerful mathematics teaching—algebra to those students thought not bright enough to master it. Ashanti requested to have these students assigned to her. Her lessons reflect her creativity and imagination as well as her deep understanding of student culture.

Ashanti teaches in a large midwestern urban school district. Her school population is a combination of poor white and poor black students. One of Ashanti's classroom activities requires the students to design a garment out of heavy-duty plastic garbage bags.

The students are required to use their algebraic skills to design and measure their fashions. The project culminates in a fashion show.

When it is time for the students' first-quarter grades, Ashanti sponsors a dinner at her home, where the students and their parents come to celebrate their hard work. She even provides a celebratory cake. The students then sit with their parents and explain their quarter grades.

Ashanti is the embodiment of "African-centered" education. Her students see a woman of regal bearing with long flowing salt and pepper dreadlocks. Her garments are typically of African-inspired fabrics and styles. She has changed her name to reflect her cultural perspective. She regularly explains to students the role of Africans, Asians, Latinos, and Europeans in the development of mathematics. Her classroom walls are filled with affirmations and other inspirational sayings that encourage her students to work hard and be proud of who they are. The fact that despite National Board certification she wanted independent eyes to help her determine whether or not her students were learning spoke volumes about her character and commitment to educating all students.

Mabel Watson

Mabel Watson, a working-class African American woman, presided over an amazing classroom. When I met her she was teaching fifth graders in an all–African American school community. Her students came from the nearby housing projects and the modest homes surrounding the school. On the surface Mabel's class might seem like any other in the school. However, one huge difference was that Mabel had been the only teacher these children ever had. She started with most of the class when they were entered in kindergarten. Every year for five years Mabel asked the school principal to allow her to move up with her students. Thus, when they went to first grade she was their first grade teacher.

When they went to second grade she became their second grade teacher, and so on until fifth grade. This fifth grade was one of the most accomplished group of students I have ever met. The students could recite long passages of oratory with great inflection. They posed challenging questions and solved difficult problems.

Ms. Watson arrives each morning impeccably dressed, wearing high heels. Within minutes of arriving in her classroom she slips out of her heels and moves around the class in bare feet. Each morning begins with a ritual with students sharing affirmations and intentions. One parent reported that before she enrolled her child in Ms. Watson's class she was warned that Ms. Watson would make her go to school also. Within a few weeks Ms. Watson was coaxing the mother to return to community college to complete her associate's degree. The mother did and credits Ms. Watson with giving her the courage to challenge her instructors' negative assessments that forced her to withdraw originally.

Among Ms. Watson's students was a girl who was told at six years old that her speech was so impaired that she needed intensive therapy. Ms. Watson disagreed and when I met the girl she was one of the leading orators of the class. Her mother beamed with pride as she recited a long passage from a sermon Ms. Watson had given her. Before leaving Ms. Watson's class I learned that she was trying to get permission from the school board to keep her students one more year rather than send them to the local middle school for their sixth grade year.

Verna Parker

Verna Parker is a very different kind of dreamkeeper. She is a first and second grade teacher whose own children are attending school in the district in which she teaches. Verna is an African American woman, married to a European American man, and an adoptive parent of children from around the world—Asia, Europe, and Latin America. Like many parents Verna has high aspirations for her children. Her son excelled in school. On one of her first visits to school during his high school years a teacher challenged Verna's parenthood. "You couldn't possibly be Walter's mother," the teacher remarked. Even when Verna was able to convince the teacher that she was the parent, the teacher never apologized for her mistake.

Verna's daughters are the same age and were placed in the same classroom. She grew concerned with the lack of challenge the girls were experiencing in writing. Because her son had attended this school she knew that this was a particular weakness in the school's curriculum. The girls were in third grade and the teacher argued that the kind of writing Verna insisted upon was not a part of the third grade curriculum and that Verna was being too demanding by expecting her daughters to write essays. Ultimately, the principal asked Verna not to come to the school because she was "upsetting" the teachers. The irony of this experience was that Verna was teaching children in first and second grade to do the very thing that she wanted her daughters' teacher to do for them. Before year's end Verna's six- and seven-year-old students had interviewed the mayor, the school superintendent, the police chief, and other prominent officials and had written articles about them that appeared in the local newspaper. Verna believes that children need intellectual challenges and when given them, they will rise to the level of excellence set before them.

Harry Clarkson

Harry Clarkson, a working-class African American man, turned around a group of African American and Latino students into championship debaters. I first saw his teaching on a DVD given to me by a long-time teacher friend. On the video, Harry was tough, demanding, exacting, and incredibly caring. He sought out those students that teachers felt were incapable of achieving and demonstrated that students could take on most challenges that teachers offer. He took his students to compete throughout the region and built a squad of champions. More important than the students' debate performances was the time Harry spent helping them seek out colleges and universities and scholarship opportunities.

I telephoned and e-mailed Harry to talk about his work. He explained that he and his students were in the midst of their competitive season and were traveling constantly. Also, his work was starting to receive national recognition and he was being invited to attend a well-known television program along with a group of outstanding teachers from across the nation. Harry's growing recognition was useful in helping him combat growing challenges from the district administrators. Harry's students had spoken out at a school board meeting chastising administrators and school board members for failing to attend the team's state championship victory. Harry had not planned to speak at the meeting but when he saw how forcefully his students spoke up he knew he had to join them. "If we were playing in a football or basketball championship most of you would have been there. Instead we were competing in an academic contest and not one district administrator showed up."

Perhaps Harry's boldness emanates from his previous experience as a teacher in the juvenile justice system. Harry pointed out that the students he taught in the correctional facility were ten times more challenging than the students at his high school. "I figured if I could reach the students that everyone else had given up on, then these students would be a piece of cake." In the DVD of Harry's work we see evidence of his caring nature and investment in his students. For example, some of his male students did not have suits to wear for an upcoming competition and Harry took them shopping and purchased clothes for them.

Renee Battle

I met Renee Battle, a middle-aged African American woman, through a group of researchers who were studying expert teachers. Renee was among a handful of teachers selected to create and post a Web page of her practice on the research project's Web site. Anyone who telephones Renee at home hears her wonderful voice mail message for the day. It alerts the caller to the fact that Renee is not available to take the call and then segues into a poem or proverb from some significant author, often of African or African American descent. Renee changes the poem or proverb every day.

Renee is a National Board of Professional Teaching Standards certified English teacher in a high school serving mostly African American students in a very large city. A part of her Web page showcases her facilitating a discussion with students about race and racism. In the midst of these highly charged topics we see Renee stepping back and allowing students to take over the discussion. When I have my own preservice students view this video segment they are struck by how engaged and vocal the students are. "How does she get them to talk and interact like that?" my students ask. Careful examination of the video embedded in the Web page reveals one of Renee's pedagogical techniques. She moves all of the desks and chairs to the perimeter of the room and asks all the students to come into the center of the classroom. Next she places them in small groups of three to four and the discussions began. "It's kind of hard to absent yourself from a conversation when you have to stand face to face with another person. When you sit at your desk you can put your head down, you can fiddle with stuff inside of the desk, you can check out even when you're sitting there."

My students marvel at the simplicity of Renee's solution and its brilliance. "How does she know to do that?" students ask. Renee points out that having experience helps but that the real key to her success comes from "studying" the students. Renee believes it is the teacher's responsibility to learn as much as she can about the students and their lives. When we know more about students we can make better decisions about what they need to perform at high levels.

During my last interaction with Renee she told me that she was serving as a mentor teacher for two young teachers of color at her school. She shared her fears of being held up by the novices as "the model" of teaching excellence. Renee was not interested in creating "Little Renees." Instead she hoped to guide the teachers toward their own strengths so that they would move comfortably into a practice that enhances student learning.

Karamu Hopkins

The irony of the next teacher, Karamu Hopkins, a young middle-class African American woman, is that I have known her since she was a student in a kindergarten in a school where I was doing research. I became a colleague and close friend of her mother in my first full-time academic job. I vicariously experienced her adolescent years as her mother shared the challenges of raising an African American female teenager in a culture of materialism and superficial and limited notions of what it means to be beautiful. Karamu struggled in the shadow of an older brother who was an exceptional student for whom everything seemed to come easily. She could not wait to graduate from the private high school they attended but found that attending a historically black college did not offer her the relief and comfort she sought. Finally, she attended and graduated from a regional college and later enrolled in a teacher preparation program that focused on social justice. Karamu flourished in the program, even pushing her professors to consider more radical alternatives to social inequity than typically discussed.

After completing the teacher credential program Karamu moved back to her hometown area and took a teaching position in one of the toughest urban districts in the state. There she developed a reputation for intellectually challenging the most challenging students. A graduate student from a nearby university selected her for his study on social justice teachers. Karamu presented her work at national conferences and spoke to media outlets and civic leaders about the deplorable conditions at her high school. Karamu participated in an important restructuring at her school and became the principal of the resulting small school. The young girl who struggled to find herself in high school made a concerted effort to ensure that other African American children would not struggle to have both a cultural and academic identity as she had to.

Carter Forshay

I met the young man I call Carter Forshay[1] shortly after the publication of *The Dreamkeepers*. Carter was a young middle-class African American man who aspired to be a broadcast journalist. He literally fell into teaching after moving to the west coast. He was assigned to teach third grade in a school that was hard to staff. He reported that his students absolutely hated to write and he was struggling to change their minds about writing. They often pleaded with him to give them simple (and mindless) fill-in-the-blank or circle-the-right-answer worksheets. They whined whenever he tried to get them to write more than a few sentences.

Rather than give in to their pleadings, Carter began some reflective practice that forced him to look at the things that excited and engaged him. Chief among his interests was music, and he presumed that his students would also enjoy music. Carter introduced his students to jazz and the way that composer and trumpeter Wynton Marsalis used various musical instruments to tell a story. Over a period of weeks, Carter's students developed a storyline, characters, and setting to tell the story of lost love. Their story was told with humor and pathos, and they discovered that writing could be both fun and empowering. Perhaps more important, Carter taught his students something about Black manhood.

One did not have to be a tough guy or gangster to be a man. Being smart and reading books did not mean that one was not a man. Taking responsibility and being dependable were qualities that students should admire. Even the fact that young African American men could be teachers was a new notion for some of Carter's students. His dedication and persistence with students on whom others had given up was an important statement Carter was determined to make. As a relatively new teacher he would make mistakes—all beginners do. However, he would not fail because he had given up. These third graders knew they could count on Mr. Forshay, and before the year was out they would show him that he could count on them.

Scott Nash

The next example I want to share is of a young man who seemed to be an unlikely candidate for the designation of "dreamkeeper." Scott Nash had spent his entire school career in private Catholic schools. He even chose a Catholic school for his undergraduate education. He was a white, smart, good-looking "golden boy" who was on the fast-track to law school. As he approached college graduation he learned that he was being awarded the university's highest academic award for his outstanding scholastic achievement. But something else happened to him during his senior year. In an attempt to fill a slot in his schedule he enrolled in an undergraduate education course that had a field experience requirement. In one short quarter Scott made a drastic change in his career plans.

According to Scott the experience in a local public high school convinced him that he wanted to do something that made society a better place, and he wanted to make a difference as soon as possible. I recall him saying that he called his parents late in his last quarter of school and asked them if they were sitting down. "I think they thought I was going to tell them something like I was getting married or running off to join a commune or something," he laughed. "When I told them I was not going to law school but was going to be a teacher they seemed somewhat relieved but then kept asking me if I were sure."

Scott enrolled in the post-baccalaureate teacher education program at his undergraduate school. The program had a social justice focus, and although many of the students in the program balked at what they saw as the constant focus on racial inequality (i.e., some students referred to the program as "too black"), Scott soaked it up like a sponge. He regularly asked questions about how to translate what he was learning to his high school English classes. He was a voracious reader and an analytic thinker. Scott did his student teaching in one of the largest and most diverse schools in the area. This school was the exact opposite of what he had experienced as a high school student, and he loved every moment of it.

At the end of his preparation year Scott was the only student-teacher offered a job at the high school. He gladly accepted the contract and began building an impressive career at the school. In the first year Scott reached out to his students' parents.

I remembered that we talked about the way some teachers treat high school students as if they were unattached to any adults and I decided I would not make that mistake. When Christmas break approached I sent home letters in English and Spanish and told the parents that I realized how hard it was to buy gifts for teenagers who often wanted expensive clothes and electronics. I recommended that they purchase paperback copies of the books we would be reading second semester. I assured them that their students would get school copies of the books but if they had their own copies they could highlight them, make notes in them, take them home each night and not have to worry about sharing them. I suggested that having their own books was likely to help their students academically. Within a week I had students coming up to me with scowls on their face saying, "Mr. Nash, guess what I'm getting for Christmas . . . books!" I was absolutely delighted with the parents' response. Now I never let anyone tell me the parents don't care. I know better.

By his second year Scott had created a special honors class for underrepresented students of color. He determined that the African American and Latino students were unlikely to be admitted in the traditional honors and AP courses the school offered. So he created his own "honors" program in which students could use their skill and knowledge in the arts and leadership to qualify for admittance. This new kind of challenge drew many students who previously exhibited little or no interest in academics.

By his fifth year in the school Scott had become one of the more popular English teachers and was very active in the teachers association. On one occasion Scott decided to take one of his two professional days in his own school building. Instead of attending a conference or workshop or visiting another school, Scott went into the main office, randomly selected a student's roster, and decided to follow it for the entire day. By the end of the day he was so frustrated that he met with his colleagues and told them he could not believe how utterly boring the school day was for students. How could teachers expect students to sit for five to six hours a day of mindless inactivity? Scott's indictment was not aimed at specific teachers, but rather at the direction the school had taken for all students. Because he was well-respected by his peers Scott was able to get a core of teachers to work together to improve teaching and learning for the students.

Jelani Muhammad

Kindergarten through twelfth grade teachers are not the only dreamkeepers available to us. Dr. Jelani Muhammad is a well-known African American mathematics professor. Although historically black colleges and universities enroll only 15 percent of the African American collegiate population, they produce 50 percent of the African American mathematics majors. Dr. Muhammad is responsible for hundreds of African American students receiving advanced degrees in mathematics. Dr. Muhammad earned a Ph.D. in mathematics from an Ivy League school in the mid-1950s. He was the only African American in his program.

Dr. Muhammad's reputation as a teacher and mentor is legendary. In 2000 he won a presidential award for mentoring. Students who did not believe they could handle the rigors of higher level mathematics report that Dr. Muhammad taught them in ways that were clear and explicit. Indeed, he made their mathematics learning "culturally relevant."[2] Dr. Muhammad regularly told his students about the way mathematics developed and flourished on the African continent and reminded them that mathematics was, in effect, a part of their birthright. He also helped them understand the social purposes of mathematics. Like former civil rights leader and algebra advocate Bob Moses, Dr. Muhammad insists that mathematics is a civil right.

Nellie McKay

Another dreamkeeper university teacher is the one person whose identity I will not mask—Professor Nellie McKay. Nellie was a friend and mentor to me from 1991 until her death in 2006 at the University of Wisconsin-Madison. Nellie wrote over sixty articles and essays but probably is best known to the general public for her incredible editorial collaboration with Harvard's Henry Louis Gates to produce the *Norton Anthology of African American Literature*. Much to the publisher's surprise, this work became a runaway best-seller and marked the first time a Norton anthology became a popular hit.

But, my memory of Nellie is as a teacher. In 1992 she won the University of Wisconsin's Distinguished Teaching Award. As a teacher of African American Literature and Women's Studies, she taught courses that a sizeable number of students resist. However,

Nellie had a way of reaching out and touching students regardless of their backgrounds. Her home was always open to her students. But she was not merely a teacher of "officially enrolled students"; she also taught her colleagues—particularly women of color.

Nellie, along with then chancellor Donna Shalala, organized the African American women faculty for a monthly dinner. This was no mere social event. Each month the black women faculty would gather at each other's homes, bring a dish to share, and then share our challenges of teaching on a campus where blacks were a tiny fraction of the teaching force and the student population. Nellie was our "mother." She reassured us that if we were persistent we would earn tenure and be able to make a difference on the campus.

A few years after Chancellor Shalala arrived she heard through the grapevine that Nellie had been offered a position at her alma mater, Harvard College. Immediately Donna asked Nellie to come to her office to talk. Donna was never one for mincing words and so she asked Nellie what it would take to ensure that she stayed at Wisconsin. Nellie, in her typical soft-spoken but emphatic way, did not do what 99.9 percent of our faculty colleagues do. She did not ask for more money (although I am sure she would not have turned that down out of hand). Nellie said with her slight Caribbean accent, "I want there to be enough black faculty on this campus that I don't have to like them all!" Nellie's request probably prompted (or at least reinforced) Chancellor Shalala's "Madison Plan"—an aggressive recruitment of faculty of color.

Finding Hope

These brief snapshots of teachers who invoke images of the original dreamkeepers represent a hope that we need to cling to in a time of teacher disempowerment and curriculum constraints. Teachers across the country are frustrated and angry about the way their profession has been characterized in media and public discourse. In school districts across the country public school teachers find themselves pitted against everything from choice, vouchers, private, and for-profit schools that do not have the same mandate that they do—to educate every student who walks through the door regardless of racial, cultural, linguistic, economic, or family circumstance. Teachers who want to try to be creative and innovative in the classroom often are told that a scripted curriculum and a pacing guide are the only answers for what should happen in their classrooms. The joy of helping students discover new ideas or dig deep into the truths of old knowledge is no longer available to most teachers teaching classrooms serving African American students. The terror of the test regime has made that kind of teaching and learning a luxury that few urban schools are willing to abide.

Often during my travels to speak with educators and parent groups there is a sense of pessimism regarding the enormity of the task before us. Too often people seem defeated by the constant calls for accountability that place all of the sanctions on the students and their teachers and the social disintegration that plagues urban school communities. But mine is not a message of despair. It is one of hope. Perhaps like Cornel West says, it is "hope on a tightrope" but it is still hope.[3] I remind my audiences that we are teaching the brightest, most creative children the world has ever seen. And we are teaching them in a time of amazing technology and rapid change.

As an African American I look back two centuries and recognize that I am but three generations away from slavery, two generations away from sharecropping, and one generation away from legal apartheid—state-sanctioned segregation. Yet, each of my ancestors had a hope nestled in a dream. My generation is the beginning of the fulfillment of that hope. The generations that succeed us are the culmination of that hope, and the task to place them on the path to their destiny belongs to those who would be dreamkeepers.

APPENDIX A: METHODOLOGY

The significance of this work for some readers will lie in the story of the teaching itself—the "what." For others, it will reside in its possibilities for replication and experimentation—the "how." It is for the latter group that this first appendix is intended.

The intent of the study was to document the practice of highly effective teachers of African American students. By drawing on the "wisdom of practice" of experienced and respected teachers,[1] I attempted to build a profile of effective practice that might be usable in teacher preparation and professional development.

This book is based on an ethnographic study using four components: teacher selection, teacher interviews, classroom observations and videotaping, and collective interpretation and analysis. The methodology of the study is important because it involves the kind of in-depth, ongoing "close to the classroom" observations that allow a researcher to understand the patterns and routines of the classroom.[2]

Each selected teacher was interviewed and each agreed to participate in a research collaborative that would analyze and interpret the data and work together to understand their collective expertise.

To document their work, they agreed to allow segments of their teaching to be videotaped and to have those videotapes shared by the group. The basic premise was contrary to the suggestion that expert teachers operate on an intuitive or automatic level.[3] The study assumed that, in the presence of other experts, teachers are capable of explaining and defining the exemplary practices that they observe. The study attempted to redefine the roles of researcher and "informant" and "avoid some of the pitfalls of researcher bias and distortion of cultural phenomena."[4]

The decision to conduct the research in this manner was strongly influenced by Asante's notion of "Afrocentricity"[5] and Collins's black feminist epistemology.[6]

Afrocentricism[7] is more than information or textbook knowledge about Africans and African Americans. It represents the building of a new scholarly tradition. Included in this tradition is an approach to scholarly inquiry that is "consistent with the ways in which people of African descent see and experience the world."[8] By conducting the research in a true collaborative style, the research processes and products reflected interpretations and analyses by the teachers I observed as facilitators and directors of pedagogical activity. What moved this research from merely collaborative to Afrocentric is that each participant agreed that the African American child and community were the *subjects* and not the *objects* of study. The approach throughout was to ask what could be learned from African American students and their teachers that maintains the integrity of their culture and their world view. We resisted the urge to make comparisons between African American students and white middle-class students. In short, we worked with the assumption that African American students and their parents demonstrate normative behavior and that they act rationally, making decisions that make sense. Nowhere in our deliberations did we cast students' or parents' behaviors in the language of pathology.

This departure from traditional modes of educational inquiry means that objectivity was not necessarily the priority—the priority was the authenticity and reality of the teachers' experiences. My role was to represent those experiences as accurately as possible while realizing that "no inquiry is ever without initial values, beliefs, conceptions, and driving assumptions regarding the matter under investigation."[9]

Teacher Selection

Teachers were selected for this study through a process that Foster termed "community nomination."[10] This means that researchers rely upon community members and community-sanctioned vehicles (for example, community newspapers and organizations) in order to judge people, places, and things within their own settings. Thus teachers were nominated by African American parents (in this case, all mothers) who attended local Baptist churches. After Sunday morning services, parents with school-aged children (ages seven to nineteen) were asked to meet with me. Accustomed to seeing the church as a conduit for important information about educational, political, social, cultural, and economic issues, the parents did not view this request as peculiar. My familiarity and active participation in the community also facilitated these meetings.

At these meetings parents were asked to suggest the teachers from the local elementary school district whom they believed to be effective with their children. The discussions began with parents clarifying what they meant by effective. Beyond the conventional notions of the students getting good grades, scoring well on standardized tests, graduating from high school, going on to college, and securing good jobs, the parents expressed an interest in an education that would help their children maintain a positive identification with their own culture. One parent cogently expressed this desire: "I just want him to hold his own in the classroom without forgetting his own in the community." The parents' concerns reflected their own experience of seeing high-achieving African American students become social isolates in order to succeed.

McLaren's citing of Fine's comments about high-achieving urban students confirms the reality of the problems these parents feared. Such students are characterized by "a moderate level of depression, an absence of political awareness, the presence of self-blame, low assertiveness, and high conformity."[11]

When the parents were asked whether they believed there were teachers in their neighborhood schools who met their qualifications they acknowledged that there were few but that they did exist. The qualities the parents identified in these teachers included willingness to include parents as active partners in the educative process without being patronizing and condescending; demand for academic excellence, including intellectual rigor and challenge; and ability to discipline the students without resorting to demeaning or abusive behavior. They also noted their children's enthusiasm for those classes (usually indicated by their unwillingness to stay home from school). The parents identified seventeen teachers (out of a district that included seven elementary schools and one middle school for a total of almost two hundred teachers).

To cross-check the nominations, I consulted the eight school principals (see Table A.1). In one school, where the principal's tenure was less than five years, teaching colleagues also were consulted. The principals and colleagues were asked to identify those teachers

Table A.1. A Successful Teacher Profile.

Teacher	Race	Years of Experience	College	Culture of Reference	Teaching Environment
Winston	W	40	Normal	Bi	RW/RB/UB
Valentine	B	25	HBC	B	UB/SWB/UB
Rossi	W	19	WC	W	UB/SW*/UB
Hilliard	B	15	WS	B	UB*/UB
Devereaux	B	21	WS	B	UB*/UB
Dupree	B	22	HBC	B	RB/UB
Harris	B	31	HBC	B	RB/UB*/UB
Lewis	W	12	WS	B	UB

Key

B   = Black
W   = White
HBC = Historically Black College
WC = White Catholic
WS = White State
Bi = Bicultural

RW = Rural White
UB = Urban Black
RB = Rural Black
SW = Suburban White
SWB = Suburban White/Black
*   = Private School

they believed to be most effective with African American students and the criteria they used to make the determination. Two of the criteria were the same as those of the parents: the teachers' ability to manage the class (often symbolized by the teachers' infrequent requests for principal assistance and intervention with student discipline) and improved student attendance; others included student gains on standardized tests. The principals and colleagues identified twenty-two teachers. Nine candidates were named by all—the parents, principals, and colleagues. These teachers who had been nominated by both groups made up the sample. However, when the nine teachers were approached about participating in the study, one declined because of lack of time and other personal reasons.

Teacher Interviews

Each teacher agreed to participate in an ethnographic interview.[12] Although I devised a tentative interview protocol, my intention really was simply to have a good conversation with each.

My initial interview questions were the following:

1. Tell me something about your background. When and where were you educated? When and where did you begin teaching?
2. How would you describe your philosophy of teaching? What do you believe "works?"
3. Can you think of any characteristics that African American youngsters as a group bring to the classroom?
4. What kinds of things have you done in the classroom that have facilitated the academic success of African American students?
5. How much of what you know about teaching African American children did you learn as a result of teacher training, either preservice or in-service?
6. If you could revamp teacher education so that teachers would be more effective with African American students, what changes would you make?

7. What kind of role do you believe parents play in the success of African American students? How would you describe the kinds of relationships you've had with parents of students you've taught?

8. How do you handle discipline? Are there special things that teachers of African American students should know about discipline?

9. How do you handle the possible mismatch between what you want to teach and what you have to teach with (for example, materials or supplies)?

10. How do you handle the possible mismatch between what you want to teach and what the administration (building principal or district superintendent) wants you to teach (for example, curricular mandates, philosophies)?

11. How do you think the schooling experience of the students you teach differs from that of white students in middle-class communities?

Although each teacher was asked and answered all the interview questions, individual teachers emphasized different questions. Some spoke extensively about their backgrounds and early schooling experiences. Others talked more about contemporary concerns. Different follow-up questions were asked of all teachers, depending on the kinds of answers the teachers had originally given.

Each interview was taped and later transcribed. The teachers were given a copy of the transcript and asked to check for errors in either fact or intent. The edited interviews were then retyped. The interviews were coded, using the computer program Ethnograph to look for key words and phrases. Then the interviews were hand-coded, searching for themes relating to pedagogy and culture. Through this coding process, I was able to arrive at an inductive model of culturally relevant teaching characteristics. Because of the tentative nature of this model and the fear of undue influence on the teachers' behavior and ongoing conversations with me, I did not use the term "culturally relevant" with them at this point in the study; I did not give them the coded interviews for the same reasons.

Each teacher received a set of all eight transcribed interviews. The interviews would provide a starting point for our first group meeting. It was at this meeting that we talked as a group about the nature of our work together. The teachers supported the idea that they would form a research collective in which their expertise would define their practice, and in which they would interpret and analyze each other's videotaped teaching.

Classroom Observations

Classroom observations took place from September 1989 to June 1991. We attempted to create a schedule for my visits, but the teachers also agreed to unscheduled visits. Because of special projects or programs longer visits were sometimes necessary, while at other times they led to a cancellation.

Observations usually lasted from ninety minutes to two hours. I tried to visit for either a morning or an afternoon. This schedule allowed me to visit each classroom at least once a week. Over the course of the study, I made approximately thirty visits to each classroom. To two of the classes (Lewis's and Devereaux's), I made an additional twenty visits for a more focused study of the literacy programs.

Audiotaped and written field notes were taken during the visits, then rewritten immediately afterward. Classroom observations were also followed by on-site conferences with the individual teacher when possible. In a few instances, the postobservation conference took place over the telephone on the evening of the observation.

As a university-based researcher I functioned as a participant-observer in the classroom. In this role sometimes I served as tutor or teacher's aide and student group member. Within a few months, I developed a certain rapport with each class and my presence did not appear to be a distraction from the regular routine and activities.

During the spring of 1990 I began to videotape classroom activities. At first the teachers were reluctant to be videotaped but agreed to do so with the stipulation that the tapes would not be viewed outside of our research group. I started by letting the tape run throughout the observation; later I selected segments of teaching practice for reviewing by the research collective. I did not rearrange elements in the classroom to enhance the quality of the videotapes (for example, to get better lighting and so on) because I wanted to minimize the camera's obtrusiveness. Thus the visual quality of the tapes is mediocre. However the teaching practices were visible enough for the purposes of our group.

Collective Interpretation and Analysis

Interpreting and analyzing the data from this research was exciting and frustrating and ultimately very productive. It helped me to rethink what I meant by *research*. I questioned my role as researcher and developed a greater respect for the expertise of the teachers. In a challenge to Berliner's notion of automaticity among experts,[13] I posited that even though experts may operate on an intuitive and automatic level, the presence of other experts might make it possible for them to describe their practices.

Although I had met with each teacher individually to interview her, watch her teach, and hold postobservation conferences, our initial group meetings reminded me of something filmmaker Spike Lee said about a scene in his movie *Jungle Fever*. This scene involved a group of African American women lamenting over the interest African American men express in white women. It is regarded as one of the most realistic scenes in the film. Lee said that rather than try to script the scene, he allowed the actresses to speak spontaneously about a subject they had real feelings about.

During our first meetings, we talked about philosophical and theoretical beliefs about teaching, the students, and the curriculum. Each teacher brought her set of transcribed interviews and often made direct references to something another teacher had said in her interview.

By the third meeting, I had several videotapes of some of the participants to share with the group. During this phase of the research, I was still involved in observing and videotaping the teachers while the group was beginning to analyze and interpret these tapes.

We had an opportunity for ten meetings to view videotaped teaching segments and offer analysis and interpretation. Near the end of the project, we had two additional meetings to talk about what we had learned and the value of this kind of professional collaboration.

Every so often a teacher suggested that she did not remember something shown on the tape or did not know why she had done it. Each time this happened another teacher (or teachers) offered a suggestion. These suggestions helped the teachers to rethink their practices and confirm or disconfirm the suggested explanation. Slowly we began building a teaching model that matched the inductive model that had come from the analysis of the interview data. As a cross-check of the model, I devised a questionnaire with a five-point Likert scale in which the members of the study rated (from "strongly agree" to "strongly disagree") positive statements about culturally relevant and assimilationist teaching practices. (For example, there was a statement on the questionnaire that read, "I believe all children can succeed" and another statement further down in the questionnaire that read, "No matter how hard I try, there always are some students I cannot reach.") As expected, the teachers scored high on the culturally relevant end of the questionnaire. This more quantitative measure served as a confirmation of the qualitative analysis.

Self-Critique

The decision to work collectively with these teachers was a reaffirmation of my commitment to conduct research in ways that honor the participants and benefit African Americans. As a researcher collecting data on expert teachers, I had to be willing to trust their judgments about their practice. Because all were knowledgeable about African American culture I was able to allow African American norms, values, and communication styles to help shape the enterprise. Thus our conversations were generally animated, with participants overlapping, interrupting, and completing one another's responses. The conventions of African American communication and civility meant that the initial stages of our collaborative meetings always involved personal talk. However, the group expected me to keep everyone on-task and to pose probing questions if we got stuck during analysis. The group evaluated the collective research experience as positive—indeed as a form of professional development more valuable than any they had previously experienced.

Although I considered this a valuable and successful research project, there is always a period of rethinking and reconsideration. I wonder how I might have done it differently. For instance, I could have kept all of my observations focused on one subject area, such as literacy. However, because I was a sole researcher observing eight classrooms I had to observe whenever I could. This meant that observations took place either in the morning or in the afternoon; thus a variety of subjects were taught when I observed.

On the positive side, I believe that studying the collective of eight teachers was far more fruitful than focusing on the practice of one or two teachers. In addition to the study of the teachers and their pedagogy, my interest in new methodologies or new ways of researching was equally strong. Sometimes researchers take their methodology as a given, as if there were no other way to answer their question. However, throughout this study I continued to ask myself whether or not there were better ways to collect information about teaching. I was overwhelmed by how carefully the teachers thought out their practices and how cogently they talked about them. I was disappointed at how little of their "wisdom of practice" has found its way into teacher preparation literature. The current demographic figures on teaching reported by the National Education Association indicate that African American teachers constitute less than 5 percent of public school teachers. Therefore, it is more important than ever to capture this practice in order to build a knowledge base of effective pedagogical practice for African American students.

Theoretical Considerations

Although researchers usually begin their works with an explanation of their theoretical position, I elected to place much of that discussion here at the end of the book for two reasons. First, some readers are less interested in the theory because it may obscure the practice and shroud it in rhetoric. Second, some readers may see the theory as a way to delimit the research and then refuse to entertain those questions and events that are inconsistent with the theory. For example, a researcher who declares her work to be in the critical theory tradition may be called to task for entertaining more interpretivist or Marxist notions.

The theoretical underpinnings of my research are what Collins terms an "Afrocentric feminist epistemology."[14] This epistemology is characterized by the following: (1) A basis of concrete experience as a criterion of meaning, (2) the use of dialogue, (3) an emphasis on caring, and (4) an emphasis on personal accountability.

A Basis of Concrete Experience

This first characteristic, as it relates to Afrocentric feminist theory, suggests that only black women can truly know what it is to be a black woman. As simplistic as this may sound, its import should not be minimized. It underscores the significance of "two types of knowing—knowledge and wisdom. . . . For most African American women, those individuals who have lived through the experiences about which they claim to be experts are more believable and credible than those who have merely read or thought about such experience."[15] In the context of this study, the concrete experiences of the teachers have primacy over theories. Teaching is explained by those who teach; in this case, by those who teach well.

The Use of Dialogue

Creating equal relationships through dialogue is another important characteristic of this theory. "Dialogue implies talk between two subjects, not the speech of subject and object. It is a humanizing speech, one that challenges and resists domination."[16] By "talking with" rather than "talking to" other black women, African American women have the opportunity to deconstruct the specificity of their own experiences and make connections with the collective experiences of others. The give and take of dialogue makes struggling together for meaning a powerful experience in self-definition and self-discovery. Casey's work detailing teachers' life histories is based solely on analysis of teachers' dialogue.[17]

For this study, dialogue was used and valued. From my early discussions with parents, to the ethnographic interviews, to the conversations among the group of teachers, dialogue led to knowledge. The dialogue was both explanatory and liberating. It allowed the teachers to view themselves in a variety of positions—as teacher, critic, expert, student, friend.

An Emphasis on Caring

White feminists have identified caring as a hallmark of women's scholarship.[18] But Collins reiterates its centrality to black women's lives and scholarship. "The ethic of caring suggests that personal expressiveness, emotions, and empathy are central to the knowledge validation process."[19] She points out that these convergent notions about caring of white and black women do not negate its importance in developing and understanding an Afrocentric feminist epistemology: "The convergence of Afrocentric and feminist values in the ethic of caring seems particularly acute. White women may have access to a women's tradition valuing emotion and expressiveness, but few Eurocentric institutions except the family validate this way of knowing. In contrast, black women have long had the support of the black church, an institution with deep roots in the African past and a philosophy that accepts expressiveness and an ethic of caring."[20]

Each participant in this study exhibited the ethic of caring. Even though the group was an integrated one, of blacks and whites, all demonstrated this ethic of caring. I believe there are at least two explanations for this. Because all were women, the importance of caring was expressed both implicitly and explicitly. For example, they talked about how much they cared about what happened to the students, and during my classroom observations I saw the ways in which they cared about the students as people. Further, because African American women made up the majority, they may have been able to "set the tone" and determine the group's cultural "ethos."

An Emphasis on Personal Accountability

The final characteristic of Afrocentric feminist epistemology suggests that claims to knowledge must be grounded in the individual. The dispassionate, "objective," white male discourse allows people with radically differing status to socialize and mingle in private; in contrast, an Afrocentric feminist epistemology brings private qualities to bear on public standpoints. Thus both *what* was said, and *who* said it give meaning and interpretation to claims.

Collins states the following: "The ethic of personal account-ability is clearly an Afrocentric value, but is it feminist as well? . . . There is a female model for moral development whereby women are more inclined to link morality to responsibility, re-lationships, and the ability to maintain social ties. If this is the case, then African American women again experience a conver-gence of values from Afrocentric and female institutions."[21]

The parents' prominent role in determining which teachers represented the standard of excellence is a testament to this no-tion of personal accountability. Further, during the time that the teachers and I met together, they began to depend on and trust one another's judgment in naming and explaining their techniques. Rather than have a researcher tell them what they were doing or what they should be doing, they relied on the perspectives of their peers in conjunction with their own pedagogical judgments. Hearing other excellent teachers speak to each teacher's practice proved to be one of the most valuable experiences of the study.

APPENDIX B: CONTEXT

＊

Appendix A explained the study's methodology. But for the anthropologist, the context is equally significant. In addition, teachers and other practitioners may question whether the context of this study makes it relevant to their own work. Therefore, this appendix describes the community history in which the study was set and its sociocultural status.

Pinewood Community

The study took place in a community in Northern California. Nestled amid affluent, predominately white communities, this community, which I will call Pinewood, is an anomaly. It is a primarily low-income, African American and Mexican American community of some twenty-five thousand. Pinewood ranks among the poorest on every economic and social-service indicator. It has the lowest per capita income, the highest unemployment and underemployment rates, the highest high school dropout rate, and the highest teenage pregnancy rate in the country. It is combating a growing drug problem and a concomitant violent crime rate. But Pinewood was not always this way.

When I moved to the area in 1978, I assumed that Pinewood had developed in response to a need for domestic service workers for the affluent neighboring communities, as is often the case. However, Pinewood had developed in a very different way. From its early days it was considered to be in an economically strategic location. Bordering the coastline, it was built around one of the only viable ports in the area. As an unincorporated area in the 1800s, it was unregulated by restrictive city ordinances. It became a poultry colony, populated by chicken farmers and later by carnation growers. It was also the only place in the area where bars were permitted. It grew at the same rate as the neighboring communities.

After World War II, real estate professionals began to view Pinewood as a prime place to speculate. Thus they began to convince residents to sell their properties. To induce them to sell, they spread a rumor that African Americans were purchasing property there. To make that rumor a reality, they began distributing flyers in the black neighborhoods of the nearby urban center, urging black veterans to use their G.I. benefits to "flee the problems of the city and move to the suburbs," where they could get larger homes and better schools. The real estate agents even provided a tour bus and a free lunch to all who were willing to ride down to see Pinewood. These tours usually took place on a workday so that those available to go were often the most undesirable, the unemployed and others who were down on their luck.

Thus the buses cruised through Pinewood jam-packed with African American people. The current residents of Pinewood peered through their windows and assumed that the rumor about black people moving to Pinewood was true. "For Sale" signs began to pop up all over. The residents became so eager to sell that they often sold their homes to a real estate agent at lower than asking price. The agent, in turn, sold the house to a black family for a much higher price. The agents made a fortune turning over real estate in Pinewood.

Because it remained an unincorporated area into the 1980s, Pinewood lacked the government ordinances that would have standardized the building requirements. The earlier poultry residents wanted the freedom to have large and irregular acreage.

However, as Pinewood began to urbanize, the lack of building regulations and ordinances became a problem. While neighboring towns and cities had ordinances that required at least a hundred feet of frontage for each housing lot, in Pinewood, for the sake of profit, many hundred-foot lots were divided into two fifty-foot lots or, in some cases, into three thirty-three-foot lots. Today, a drive from the neighboring cities into Pinewood highlights the density of the housing there.

Another problem that the lack of city government created for Pinewood was an inability to stop the state from building a major highway right through the middle of the community. Most of Pinewood lay to the east of the freeway, while the few whites who stayed were on the west side, closer to the more affluent neighboring towns.

Although prohibitions on the sale of alcohol had been repealed in the neighboring towns by the 1950s, the small stretch of land that constituted Pinewood's business district became known as "Liquor Lane" and was frequented by people from throughout the area. The liquor stores, bars, and clubs were not owned by Pinewood residents.

When I moved to the area in 1978, Pinewood had one supermarket, a post office, two branches of national banks, a savings and loan, a couple of drug stores, an undertaker, a library, several barbers and beauticians, two gas stations, and a variety of fast food outlets. Before my arrival, the town had had a small shopping center in a strip mall; but by 1978, it had been abandoned and fallen victim to arson. Pinewood was still unincorporated and under the jurisdiction of the county.

In 1983, after several unsuccessful attempts, the community managed to get itself incorporated as a city. Today, the county has gradually reduced its services and the city is struggling to maintain itself on a very small tax base. Both of the banks and the savings and loan that existed earlier have closed their Pinewood branch offices. The supermarket is not a member of a major chain and its prices are not competitive. Further, it has been cited for USDA meat violations. The burned-out shopping mall is a home for vagrants and crack cocaine addicts. The post office, which is located across the street from the mall, is losing business to a newer, fully equipped postal station located in a neighboring town.

Because of the constant media attention to crime in Pinewood, conveniences such as pizza delivery are not possible. The local afflu-ent communities have successfully gerrymandered the best property of Pinewood and sold it to large companies. Thus Pinewood has within its midst corporations that pay their taxes to more afflu-ent neighboring municipalities. There is considerable acrimony between the citizens of Pinewood and those of the neighboring communities. That acrimony finds its ways into the schools.

Pinewood City Schools*

Although the first schools in the county were opened in 1852, the part of the school history most salient to Pinewood today begins in the World War II and postwar era. As with many communi-ties across the nation, World War II brought increased growth of the facilities of the Pinewood City school district. In 1942, a five-room wing was added to the one existing district school (Pinewood School) and two other schools were built. New subdivisions con-tinued to spring up from nowhere, and in the late 1940s the district, bonded to capacity, sought and received $2.5 million in state aid. In order to qualify, the board of trustees agreed to abandon or dis-pose of buildings declared unsafe by the public works departments. Land was purchased and construction began on four new schools.

---

*This information on the Pinewood City School District history is taken from my dissertation, Citizenship and Values: An Ethnographic Study of Citizenship and Values in a Predominantly Black School Setting. Unpublished dissertation, Stanford University, Stanford, Calif., 1984. The names of places and people are changed to protect confidentiality.

In the spring of 1953 the board of trustees ordered the old section of Pinewood School, the wing, and the auditorium closed to students, but the school was still used for administrative purposes and storage. Early in 1954, the district's business manager traveled to the state capitol to file the notices of completion on the buildings constructed under the state aid program. Immediately afterward, the district was informed that it had to abandon Pinewood School for all uses immediately or lose all insurance on its school buildings. Thus all of Pinewood School was vacated. Toward the end of the 1954–55 school year, another school was completed containing fourteen classrooms and administrative offices.

The period from 1955 to 1961 was one of rapid expansion in the district; Pinewood added three school buildings, bringing the total number of Pinewood schools to eleven, and thirty-two classrooms were added to various existing schools. In June 1965 construction began on a twelfth school.

In the fall 1967 the Pinewood school district hired its first African American school superintendent, Thomas Mandan. Under his leadership, a master planning committee was formed to begin comprehensive planning in the district and to implement a school program of individualized instruction where each student's educational needs were identified and met. This committee provided the framework or outline for implementing a program that required the participation of the community and parents. This framework was the basis of an innovative instructional philosophy that gave the parents more say in the school programming.

In 1971, Mandan chose Wayne Harmon as assistant superintendent. Harmon had come to the district as the principal of one of the schools in 1968. As a school principal, he had been heralded for changing the school's image from that of a "babysitting dump" to one where students really grew and learned. Under his tenure, two themes had emerged in the school: "Black is beautiful" and "Black children can learn and do learn." Harmon's growing involvement in the Pinewood community made him the logical selection as Mandan's second-in-command.

In 1972 Mandan resigned. The board of trustees appointed Harmon acting superintendent and launched a national search for a new superintendent. The political struggle that arose between the school board and the community over the selection of a new superintendent resulted in the election of an all–African American board of trustees, which subsequently appointed Harmon superintendent in July 1973.

His position now secure, Harmon, along with an African American teacher educator from the local state university, launched an ambitious new curriculum and instruction philosophy for the district. The major tenets of the program were a philosophy that demanded the input of families and the community in educational decisions; an organizational structure based on an extended family concept where every teacher was responsible for every child; students grouped in shared unit arrangements; and school–family relations that extended beyond the classroom. The new program required changes both in content and in instructional techniques. Skill development was to be aided with multicultural content and instruction was to be varied, with teachers helping students develop processes that helped them learn how to learn.

Thus the dream of educational and cultural excellence in the Pinewood City school district was born. Unfortunately, the reality fell far short of the dream. Like its surrounding community districts, Pinewood began to experience declining school enrollment at the same time that costs rose with inflation. To combat these problems the district was forced to reorganize and consolidate. In the 1973–74 school year, the district closed three schools and created one junior high complex. Now the Pinewood City school district had only six instructional sites—a day care center, a junior high, and four elementary schools.

In the 1974–75 school year the district experienced its first teacher strike, which lasted four days. In addition to a teacher strike, the district was faced with the challenge of having to back away from the second phase of its reorganization plan because of parental protests. Between 1975 and 1981 the district went through several reorganizations. It maintained six educational sites but, by 1977, four schools were K–8 schools, one became a K–3 school, and one remained a day care facility. By the 1981–82 school year, the board of trustees reorganized the district again, this time creating four K–5 schools and a middle school for sixth to eighth graders.

These reorganizations were traumatic in themselves but became even more so because of frequent changes in administration. In August 1976, Harmon requested a seven-month leave of absence to accept a doctoral fellowship at an Eastern university. At the end of that period, he refused to say if he would return to Pinewood. Both the leave of absence and his failure to respond came as surprises to the Pinewood community in light of the fierce battles that had been waged in his behalf during the struggle to name him superintendent.

Harmon's 1977 resignation meant that the board had to appoint an acting superintendent once again and begin another search for a superintendent. They brought in Dr. Lawrence Witherspoon from New York to lead the district and offered him a two-year contract. Despite Witherspoon's attempts at sweeping improvements, by his own admission, he was not politically astute and was forced to resign in February 1980, four months before his contract was to expire. He was replaced by the now-familiar acting superintendent and the search for a new leader began again. This time, Dr. William Banks, an administrator from Detroit, was chosen. Banks arrived in time to implement the district's middle-school reorganization—a reorganization fraught with problems. Before the end of the 1981–82 school year, Banks was accused of incompetence and mismanagement and was subsequently fired. Once again an acting superintendent was named and a search was instituted.

In October 1982, the board of trustees appointed Dr. Melvin
Sands superintendent. Sands had been an administrator in several districts in the southern part of the state and claimed experience with districts similar to Pinewood.

With all this change and upheaval occurring at the top level, student performance reflected the uncertainty and lack of leadership.
The district continued to be plagued with plummeting test scores
and high teacher turnover. As early as 1960, one Pinewood parent
had organized a "sneak-out" program, instructing parents on how
to secret their students out of Pinewood schools and into neighboring districts with good academic reputations. This process lasted
for years. Eventually, using an affidavit system, parents attested that
at least four nights a week their children lived with someone in a
neighboring district. A county board declared the affidavit system
illegal and called an end to the large-scale defections.

In 1981, the "Pinewood Predicament" was publicized in the
local newspaper in a series of articles. The series indicated that
almost three thousand families who lived within the district's
boundaries had opted either to send their children to private
schools or to persist in sneak-out attempts. Included among them
were children of a Pinewood board of trustees member and a former member. The problems cited by the newspaper included low
test scores, a high senior high school drop-out rate among the
district's eighth-grade graduates, high turnover in personnel, and
a grand jury investigation into the management of district funds.

The newspaper concluded that the district's poor performance
was due to its poor students—many from single-parent families.
It called for attempts to "prepare them to compete (at the high
school level) with some of the most privileged children in the
country."

Pinewood's problems were (and continue to be) well known to
state officials. As far back as 1970, the governor had to approve a measure allowing for a $600,000 loan to be made to the district because
of exorbitant budget deficits. In 1979, the state superintendent of

education was quoted as saying that the district should be abolished. When given an opportunity to clarify his statement, he said that what he meant was that district lines never should have been created to isolate a poor community from surrounding areas.

In 1983 Sands was forced to resign, and administrative stability finally came to the district in the person of an African American woman, Dr. Connie Dayton. She was well known throughout the state as a former assistant state superintendent and the superintendent of a district in another part of the state that resembled Pinewood in socioeconomic status and academic performance. Politically savvy and not afraid of stepping on toes, Dayton began exposing some of Pinewood's internal problems. Because being a paraprofessional was one of the few employment opportunities in Pinewood, the school district was "bottom heavy" with paraprofessionals, many of whom were family members and friends of administrators and board members. Dayton began a campaign to improve the district's image; she used her connections and skills to draw millions of foundation and philanthropic dollars into Pinewood. Well known to national African American leaders, she was able to bring an array of famous personalities to the district to speak at graduation and special event ceremonies.

During Dayton's tenure, a longstanding legal action finally made it to the state court of appeals. During the infamous sneak-out program, one parent, Martha Teasdale, sued the district and the eleven surrounding mostly white, affluent districts for complicity in providing inferior education to African American and Latino students. To almost everyone's surprise, the Teasdale decision was settled in favor of the plaintiff (who no longer had school-aged children). The settlement allowed parents with children in kindergarten through grade three to enter their names into a lottery to send their children to one of the surrounding, more affluent districts. At the beginning of the school year, Pinewood's superintendent would select 150 of the entries, and these parents were permitted to select the districts outside Pinewood where they wanted their children to attend. No more than 250 students were allowed to leave Pinewood under the settlement. Dayton lobbied the state to compensate Pinewood for the loss of revenue (that came from the lower average daily attendance), threatening to "hold the students hostage" if Pinewood suffered financially. The state agreed to give Pinewood $1 million to compensate for the loss of average daily attendance funds. After several years, Teasdale-decision students began returning to Pinewood. Reports of racism and discrimination by teachers and students in the neighboring district convinced many parents that going to school with rich white children was not worth the trauma.

Since its incorporation, Pinewood has struggled to combat the scourge of drugs, particularly crack cocaine. Fights over drug turf have resulted in Pinewood becoming one of the most violent cities in the country. The last two school years have seen Pinewood students killed in drive-by shootings and execution-style murders. Families have suffered (and continue to suffer) tremendous stress. More and more grandmothers have become responsible for rearing their children's children. The school district has become a more central player in the nurturing of many children; the lucky ones end up in classes where culturally relevant teaching is practiced.

A Final Note About the Teachers

Five of the eight teachers in this study had a long tenure in Pinewood. They witnessed and were victimized by the frequent squabbles and administrator shifts. They saw what drugs and state and federal neglect did to the community. They stayed in Pinewood because they wanted to, not because they had to. Each was offered the opportunity to teach in a more affluent, less stressful school environment. But for all of them, teaching in Pinewood remains a calling—a chance to be active participants in the construction of a dream.

NOTES

*

Foreword to the New Edition

1. My colleagues in London, Melbourne, Australia, and Umeå, Sweden, have used this book in their classes.
2. This study resulted in the book, Ladson-Billings, G., *Crossing Over to Canaan: The Journey of New Teachers in Diverse Classrooms*. San Francisco: Jossey-Bass, 2001.

Chapter One

1. Du Bois, W. B. "Does the Negro Need Separate Schools?" *Journal of Negro Education*, 1935, 4, 328–335.
2. Murrell, P. "Afrocentric Immersion: Academic and Personal Development of African American Males in Public Schools." In T. Perry and J. Fraser, *Freedom's Plow: Teaching in Multicultural Classrooms*. New York: Routledge & Kegan Paul, 1993, 231–256.
3. Bray, R. "The Miseducation of Our Children." *Essence*, Sept. 1987, pp. 79–80, 153–156.
4. Edelman, M. *Families in Peril: An Agenda for Social Change*. Cambridge, Mass.: Harvard University Press, 1987.
5. Chan, V., and Momparler, M. "George Bush's Report Card: What's He Got Against Kids?" *Mother Jones*, May/June 1991, pp. 44–45.
6. Kunjufu, J. *Developing Discipline and Positive Self-Images in Black Children*. Chicago: Afro-American Images, 1984.

7. The first wave of educational reform was initiated by the Commission on Excellence in Education's *A Nation at Risk* and was aimed largely at school improvement. The second wave, ushered in by the Holmes Group report *Teachers for Tomorrow's Schools* and the Carnegie report *A Nation Prepared: Teachers for the Twenty-First Century*, focused on teacher reform.

8. Harlan, S. "Compared to White Children, Black Children are . . ." *USA Today*, June 5, 1985, p. 9A.

9. Chan and Momparler, "George Bush's Report Card," p. 44.

10. "Saving Our Schools." *Fortune*, Spring 1990 (special issue).

11. Murrell, P. "Our Children Deserve Better." *Rethinking Schools*, Dec./Jan. 1988, 2(2), 1, 4, 15.

12. Ratteray, J. D. *What's in a Norm: How African Americans Score on Achievement Tests*. Washington, D.C.: Institute for Independent Education, 1989.

13. Ratteray, J. D. *Access to Quality: Private Schools in Chicago's Inner City*. Heartland Policy Study, no. 9. Chicago: Heartland Institute, 1986.

14. Lowe, R. "The Struggle for Equal Education: An Historical Note." *Rethinking Schools*, Dec./Jan. 1988, 2(2), 5.

15. Irvine, J. "Black Parents' Perceptions of Their Children's Desegregated School Experiences." Paper presented at the annual meeting of the American Educational Research Association, Boston, Mass., April 1990.

16. Du Bois, W.E.B. "Perchstein and Pecksniff." *Crisis*, Sept. 1929, 36, 313–314.

17. Fleming, J. *Blacks in College*. San Francisco: Jossey-Bass, 1984.

18. See, for example, Bacon, M. "High-Potential Students from Ravenswood Elementary School District (Follow-Up Study)," unpublished report to the Sequoia Union High School District, Redwood City, Calif., 1981; and Lomotey, K., and Staley, J. "The Education of African Americans in the Buffalo Public Schools: An Exploratory Study," paper presented at

the annual meeting of the American Educational Research Association, Boston, Mass., April 1990.

19. Lomotey, K., and Staley, J. "The Education of African Americans."

20. Bell, D. *And We Are Not Saved: The Elusive Quest for Racial Justice*. New York: Basic Books, 1987.

21. McPartland, J. "The Relative Influence of School and of Classroom Desegregation on the Academic Achievement of Ninth-Grade Negro Students." *Journal of Social Issues*, 1969, 25(3), 93–103.

22. Grant, C., and Secada, W. "Preparing Teachers for Diversity." In W. R. Houston (ed.), *Handbook of Research on Teacher Education*. New York: Macmillan, 1990, 403–422.

23. Ladson-Billings, G. "Who Will Teach Our Children: Preparing Teachers to Successfully Teach African American Students." In E. Hollins, J. King, and W. Hayman (eds.), *Building the Knowledge Base for Teaching Culturally Diverse Learners*. Albany, N.Y.: State University of New York Press, 1994.

24. For examples see Bloom, B., Davis, A., and Hess, R., *Compensatory Education for Cultural Deprivation*. Troy, Mo.: Holt, Rinehart & Winston, 1965; Bettelheim, B., "Teaching the Disadvantaged," *National Education Association Journal*, 1965, 54, 8–12; Ornstein, A., and Vairo, P. (eds.), *How to Teach Disadvantaged Youth*, New York: McKay, 1968; Ornstein, A., "The Need for Research on Teaching the Disadvantaged," *Journal of Negro Education*, 1971, 40(2), 133–139.

25. For examples of this literature see Austin, G., "Exemplary Schools and the Search for Effectiveness," *Educational Leadership*, 1979, 37, 10–14; Brookover, W. B., and Lezotte, L. "Changes in School Characteristics Coincident with Changes in Student Achievement," unpublished paper, Michigan State University, 1979 (ERIC ED 181 005); and Edmonds, R., "Effective Schools for the Urban Poor," *Educational Leadership*, 1970, 37, 15–24.

26. Cohen, E., and Benton, J. "Making Groupwork Work." *American Educator*, Fall 1988, pp. 10–17, 45–46.

27. Ladson-Billings, G., "Who Will Teach Our Children," pp. 129–142.

28. Bloom, B., Davis, A., and Hess, R., *Compensatory Education*.

29. Bettelheim, 1965; Ornstein and Vairo, 1968; Ornstein, 1971; Doll, R., and Hawkins, M., *Educating the Disadvantaged*. New York: AMS Press, 1971; Hyram, G., *Challenge to Society: The Education of the Culturally Disadvantaged Child*, Vol. 1, New York: Pagent-Poseidon, Ltd., 1972.

30. Mitchell, J. "Reflections of a Black Social Scientist: Some Struggles, Some Doubts, Some Hopes." *Harvard Educational Review*, 1982, *52*, 27–44.

31. Cuban, L. "The 'At-Risk' Label and the Problem of Urban School Reform." *Phi Delta Kappan*, 1989, *70*, 780–784, 799–801.

32. Hollins, E. R. "A Reexamination of What Works for Inner City Black Children." Paper presented at the annual meeting of the American Educational Research Association, Boston, Mass., April 1990.

33. Levine, D., and Stark, J. "Instructional and Organizational Arrangements that Improve Achievement in Inner-City Schools." *Educational Leadership*, Dec. 1982, pp. 41–46.

34. Comer, J. "New Haven's School-Community Connection." *Educational Leadership*, Mar. 1987, pp. 13–16.

35. Hollins, E. R. "A Conceptual Framework for Selecting Instructional Approaches and Materials for Inner City Black Youngsters." Paper commissioned by the California Curriculum Commission Ad Hoc Committee on Special Needs Students, Sacramento, Calif., March 1989, p. 15.

36. Cummins, J. "Empowering Minority Students." *Harvard Educational Review*, 1986, *17*(4), 18–36.

37. Au, K., and Jordan, C. "Teaching Reading to Hawaiian Children: Finding a Culturally Appropriate Solution."

In H. Trueba, G. Guthrie, and K. Au (eds.), *Culture and the Bilingual Classroom: Studies in Classroom Ethnography*. Rowley, Mass.: Newbury House, 1981, 139–152.

38. Hollins, E. R. "The Marva Collins Story Revisited." *Journal of Teacher Education*, 1982, 32(1), 37–40.

39. See, for example, Fordham, S., and Ogbu, J., "Black Students' School Success: Coping with the Burden of 'Acting White,'" *The Urban Review*, 1986, 18(3), 1–31; Bacon, 1981; McLaren, P., *Life in Schools: An Introduction to Critical Pedagogy in the Foundations of Education*. White Plains, N.Y.: Longman, 1989.

40. Kohl, H. *I Won't Learn from You! The Role of Assent in Learning*. Minneapolis: Milkweed Editions, 1991.

41. See Hirshberg, C., "Bayton's Boys Do the Right Thing," *Life*, Sept. 1991, pp. 24–28, 30, 32; and Holland, S., "Positive Primary Education for Young Black Males," *Education Week*, Mar. 25, 1987, 6, 24.

42. Eisner, E. "The Art and Craft of Teaching." *Educational Leadership*, 1982, 40, 4–13.

43. Giroux, H., and Simon, R. "Popular Culture and Critical Pedagogy: Everyday Life as a Basis for Curriculum Knowledge." In P. McLaren and H. Giroux, (eds.), *Critical Pedagogy, the State, and Cultural Struggle*. Albany, N.Y.: State University of New York Press, 1989, 236–252.

Chapter Two

1. Mohatt, G., and Erickson, F. "Cultural Differences in Teaching Styles in an Odawa School: A Sociolinguistic Approach." In H. Trueba, G. Guthrie, and K. Au (eds.), *Culture and the Bilingual Classroom: Studies in Classroom Ethnography*. Rowley, Mass.: Newbury House, 1981, 105–119.

2. Au, K., and Jordan, C. "Teaching Reading to Hawaiian Children: Finding a Culturally Appropriate Solution."

In H. Trueba, G. Guthrie, and K. Au, (eds.), *Culture and the Bilingual Classroom: Studies in Classroom Ethnography.* Rowley, Mass.: Newbury House, 1981, 139–152.

3. See, for example, Cazden, C., and Leggett, E., "Culturally Responsive Education: Recommendations for Achieving Lau Remedies II," in H. Trueba, G. Guthrie, and K. Au, (eds.), *Culture and Bilingual Classrooms: Studies in Classroom Ethnography,* Rowley, Mass.: Newbury House, 1981, 69–86; and Erickson, F., and Mohatt, G., "Cultural Organization and Participation Structures in Two Classrooms of Indian Students," in Spindler, G. (ed.), *Doing the Ethnography of Schooling,* Troy, Mo.: Holt, Rinehart & Winston, 1982, 131–174.

4. See, for example, Jordan, C. "Translating Culture: from Ethnographic Information to Educational Program," *Anthropology and Education Quarterly,* 1985, 16(2), 105–123; and Vogt, L., Jordan, C., and Tharp, R., "Explaining School Failure, Producing School Success: Two Cases." *Anthropology and Education Quarterly,* 1987, 18(4), 276–286.

5. Villegas, A. "School Failure and Cultural Mismatch: Another View. *The Urban Review,* 1988, 20(4), 253–265.

6. Giroux, H. *Theory and Resistance in Education.* South Hadley, Mass.: Bergin & Garvey, 1983.

7. McLaren, P. *Life in Schools: An Introduction to Critical Pedagogy in the Foundations of Education.* White Plains, N.Y.: Longman, 1989.

8. See, for example, Asante, M. K., *The Afrocentric Idea,* Philadelphia: Temple University Press, 1987; King, J., and Mitchell, C., *Mothers to Sons: Juxtaposing African American Literature with Social Practice,* New York: Peter Lang, 1991.

9. Hale-Benson, J. *Black Children: Their Roots, Culture, and Learning Styles.* Baltimore, Md.: Johns Hopkins University Press, 1986.

10. Taylor, D., and Dorsey-Gaines, C. *Growing Up Literate: Learning from Inner-City Families.* Portsmouth, N.H.: Heinemann Educational Books, 1988.

11. See, for example, Heath, S. B., *Ways with Words: Language, Life, and Work in Communities and Classrooms*. Cambridge, England: Cambridge University Press, 1983; and Gee, J. P., "Literacy, Discourse, and Linguistics: Introduction." *Journal of Education*, 1989, *171*(1), 5–25.

12. Irvine, J. *Black Students and School Failure*. Westport, Conn.: Greenwood Press, 1990.

13. Irvine, J. "Cultural Responsiveness in Teacher Education: Strategies to Prepare Majority Teachers for Successful Instruction of Minority Students." Paper presented at the annual meeting of Project 30, Monterey, Calif., Dec. 1–4, 1989, p. 4.

14. Ladson-Billings, G. "Like Lightning in a Bottle: Attempting to Capture the Pedagogical Excellence of Successful Teachers of Black Students." *The International Journal of Qualitative Studies in Education*, 1990, *3*(4), 335–344.

15. King, J. "Unfinished Business: Black Student Alienation and Black Teachers' Emancipatory Pedagogy." In Foster, M. (ed.), *Readings in Equal Education*. New York: AMS Press, 1991a, pp. 245–271.

16. Ladson-Billings, G., and King, J. *Cultural Identity of African Americans: Implications for Achievement*. Aurora, Colo.: Mid-Continental Regional Educational Laboratory (McREL), 1990.

17. See, for example, Crano, W., and Mellon, P., "Causal Influences of Teachers' Expectations on Children's Academic Performance: A Cross-Lagged Panel Analysis," *Journal of Educational Psychology*, 1978, *70*(1), 39–44; Cooper, H., "Pygmalion Grows Up: A Model for Teacher Expectation Communication and Performance Influence." *Review of Educational Research*, 1979, *49*(3), 389–410; and Smith, M., "Metanalyses of Research on Teacher Expectation." *Evaluation in Education*, 1980, *4*, 53–55.

18. Winfield, L. "Teacher Beliefs Toward At-Risk Students in Inner Urban Schools." *The Urban Review*, 1986, *18*(4), 253–267.

19. Ladson-Billings, G., and King, J. *Cultural Identity of African Americans: Implications for Achievement*. Aurora, Colo.: Midcontinental Regional Educational Laboratory, 1990.

20. Shulman, L. "Those Who Understand: Knowledge Growth in Teaching." *Educational Researcher*, 1986, *15*(4), 4–14.

21. Ladson-Billings, "Like Lightning in a Bottle," pp. 335–344.

22. Ladson-Billings, G. "Is Eight Enough: Pedagogical Reflections of Eight Successful Teachers of Black Students." Paper presented at the Wisconsin Center for Educational Research, Visiting Minority Scholars Program, Mar. 1990.

23. Lightfoot, S. L. *The Good High School: Portraits of Character and Culture*. New York: Basic Books, 1983.

24. Over the course of the study, I noted that this teacher, who was relatively new to the district, developed closer relationships with African American teachers and other school personnel. By year three she was regularly attending a weight-loss program with her African American principal.

Chapter Three

1. Paley, V. G. *White Teacher*. Cambridge, Mass.: Harvard University Press, 1979.

2. Delpit, L. "Seeing Color." *Rethinking Schools*. Jan./Feb. 1991, *5*(2), 5–6.

3. King, J. "Dysconscious Racism: Ideology, Identity, and the Miseducation of Teachers." *Journal of Negro Education*, 1991, *60*(2), 133–146.

4. King, J., and Ladson-Billings, G. "The Teacher Education Challenge in Elite University Settings: Developing Critical Perspectives for Teaching in Democratic and Multicultural Societies." *European Journal of Intercultural Education*, 1990, *1*(2), 15–30.

5. Foster, H. *Ribbin, Jivin', and Playin' the Dozens*. (2nd ed.) New York: Ballinger, 1986.

6. "The Truth About Teachers." Videotape. Santa Monica, Calif.: Pyramid Film and Video, 1989.

7. Mrs. Valentine transferred to another district school in the second year of the study. Her husband's job transferred him out of the area, and she left the school district.

8. Spindler, G. "Roger Harker and Schonhausen: From the Familiar to the Strange and Back Again." In Spindler, G., *Doing the Ethnography of Schooling*, Prospect Heights, Ill.: Waveland Press, 1982, pp. 20–46.

9. Hare, B., and Castenell, L. A. "No Place to Run, No Place to Hide: Comparative Status and Future Prospects of Black Boys." In Spencer, M. B., Brookins, G. K., and Allen, W. R. (eds.), *Beginnings: The Social and Affective Development of Black Children*, Hillsdale, N.J.: Erlbaum 1985, pp. 201–214.

10. Foster, *Ribbin, Jivin*, pp. 297–298.

Chapter Four

1. Jackson, P. *Life in Classrooms*. Troy, Mo.: Holt, Rinehart & Winston, 1968.

2. Dreeben, R. *On What Is Learned in School*. Reading, Mass.: Addison-Wesley, 1968.

3. Rist, R. "Student Social Class and Teacher Expectations: The Self-Fulfilling Prophecy in Ghetto Education." *Harvard Educational Review*, 1970, 40, 411–451.

4. Spindler, G. "Roger Harker and Schonhausen: From the Familiar to the Strange and Back Again." In G. Spindler (ed.), *Doing the Ethnography of Schooling*. Prospect Heights, Ill.: Waveland Press, 1982.

5. Slavin, R. "Cooperative Learning and the Cooperative School." *Educational Leadership*, 1987, 45, 7–13.

6. Wilson, T. L. "Notes Toward a Process of Afro-American Education." *Harvard Educational Review*, 1972, 42, 374–389.

7. See, for example, Foster, M., "Constancy, Connectedness and Constraints in the Lives of African American Women Teachers." *National Association of Women's Studies Journal*, 1991, 3(2), 70–97; and Murrell, P. "Cultural Politics in Teacher Education." In M. Foster (ed.), *Readings on Equal Education*, Vol. 11. New York: AMS Press, 1991, pp. 205–225.

8. See for example, Rist, "Student Social Class," p. 449; Spindler, 1982, p. 29.

9. Ladson-Billings, G. "Returning to the Source: Implications for Educating Teachers of Black Students." In M. Foster (ed.), *Readings in Equal Education*, Vol. 11. New York: AMS Press, 1991, pp. 227–244.

10. Dreeben, *On What Is Learned in School*, p. 23.

11. Nobles, W. "Psychological Research and the Black Self-Concept: A Critical Review." *Journal of Social Issues*, 1973, 29(1), 11–31.

12. See, for example Cohen, E., and Benton, J., "Making Groupwork Work." *American Educator*, Fall 1988, pp. 10–17, 45–46; and Slavin, R., and Madden, N., "What Works for Students at Risk: A Research Synthesis." *Educational Leadership*, 1988, 46(5), 4–13.

13. See, for example, Raths, L., Harmin, M., and Simon, S., *Values and Teaching: Working with Values in the Classroom* (2nd ed.). Columbus, Ohio: Merrill, 1978; and Simon, S., Howe, L., and Kirschenbaum, H., *Values Clarification: A Handbook of Practical Strategies for Teachers and Students*. New York: Hart, 1972.

Chapter Five

1. Kuhn, T. *The Structure of Scientific Revolutions*. (2nd ed., enlarged). Chicago: University of Chicago Press.

2. Hughes, R. "The Fraying of America." *Time*, Feb. 3, 1992, pp. 44–49.

3. Graff, G. *Beyond the Culture Wars*. New York: W. W. Norton, 1992.

4. Bloom, A. *The Closing of the American Mind: How Higher Education Has Failed Democracy and Impoverished the Souls of Today's Students*. New York: Simon & Schuster, 1987.

5. Hirsch, E. D. *Cultural Literacy: What Every American Needs to Know*. Boston: Houghton Mifflin, 1987.

6. Cornbleth, C., and Waugh, D. "The Great Speckled Bird: Education Policy-in-the-Making." *Educational Researcher*, 1993, 22(7), 31–37.

7. Ladson-Billings, G. "Distorting Democracy: An Ethnographic Description of the California History-Social Science Textbook Adoption Process." Paper presented at the annual meeting of the American Educational Research Association, San Francisco, April 1992.

8. Apple, M. "Is There a Curriculum Voice to Reclaim?" *Phi Delta Kappan*, 1990, 71(7), 526–530.

9. Janko, E. "Knowing Is Not Thinking." *Phi Delta Kappan*, 1989, 70(7), 543–544.

10. Delpit, L. "Skills and Other Dilemmas of a Progressive Black Educator." *Harvard Educational Review*, 1986, 56, 379–385.

11. Lipman, P. "Influence of School Restructuring on Teachers' Beliefs and Practices with African American Students." Unpublished doctoral dissertation. Madison, Wis.: University of Wisconsin, 1993.

12. Gibson, R. *Critical Theory and Education*. Suffolk, England: Hodder and Stoughton, 1986.

13. Shulman, L. "Knowledge and Teaching: Foundations of the New Reform." *Harvard Educational Review*, 1987, 57(1), 9.

Chapter Six

1. Amove, R., and Graff, H. "National Literacy Campaigns: Historical and Comparative Lessons." *Phi Delta Kappan*, 1987, 69(3), 202–206.

214 NOTES

2. Ferdman, B. "Literacy and Cultural Identity." *Harvard Educational Review,* 1990, 60(2), 181–204.
3. deCastell, S., and Luke, A. "Defining Literacy in North American Schools: Social and Historical Conditions and Consequences." *Journal of Curriculum Studies,* 1983, 15, 373–389.
4. Gadsden, V. (ed.). "Literacy and the African American Learner." *Theory into Practice,* 1991, 31(4), 275.
5. For further elaboration of these tenets, see Ladson-Billings, G. "Liberatory Consequences of Literacy." *The Journal of Negro Education,* 1992, 61, 378–391.
6. Spradley, J. *The Ethnographic Interview.* Troy, Mo.: Holt, Rinehart & Winston, 1979.
7. The summary statements on pp. 186–190 are taken from Ladson-Billings, G., "Making Math Meaningful in Cultural Contexts." In W. Secada, E. Fenemma, and L. Byrd (eds.), *New Dimensions in Equity.* New York: Cambridge University Press, 1994.

Chapter Seven

1. Kozol, J. *Savage Inequalities.* New York: Crown, 1991, p. 51.
2. Bell, D. *Faces at the Bottom of the Well: The Permanence of Racism.* New York: Basic Books, 1992, 198.
3. Lipman, P. "Influence of School Restructuring on Teachers' Beliefs and Practices with African American Students." Unpublished doctoral dissertation. Madison, Wis.: University of Wisconsin, 1993.
4. Grant, C., and Secada, W. "Preparing Teachers for Diversity." In W. R. Houston (ed.), *Handbook of Research on Teacher Education.* New York: Macmillan, 1990, 403–422.
5. Ahlquist, R. "Position and Imposition: Power Relations in a Multicultural Foundations Class." *The Journal of Negro Education,* 1990, 60(2), 158–169.
6. Grant, C. "Urban Teachers: Their New Colleagues and Curriculum." *Phi Delta Kappan,* 1989, 70(10), 764–770.

7. Haberman, M. "More Minority Teachers." *Phi Delta Kappan*, 1989, *70*(10), 771–776.

8. Sizer, T. *Horace's School: Redesigning the American High School*. Boston: Houghton Mifflin, 1992.

9. Bennett, W. *James Madison High School: A Curriculum for American Students*. Washington, D.C.: U.S. Department of Education, 1987.

10. Cartwright, M., with D'Orso, M. *For the Children*. New York: Doubleday, 1993.

Afterword

1. I wrote about Carter's work in an earlier volume: Ladson-Billings, G. "I ain't writin' nuttin': Permissions to Fail and Demands to Succeed in Urban Classrooms." In L. Delpit and J. Dowdy, (Eds.), *The Skin That We Speak: Thoughts on Language and Culture in the Classroom*. New York: The Free Press, 1992.

2. Ladson-Billings, G. *The Dreamkeepers: Successful Teachers of African American Children*. San Francisco: Jossey-Bass, 1994.

3. West, C. *Hope on a Tightrope: Words and Wisdom*. Carlsbad, Calif.: Smiley Books, 2008.

Appendix A

1. Shulman, L. "Knowledge and Teaching: Foundations of the New Reform." *Harvard Educational Review*, 1987, *57*(1), 1–22.

2. Shulman, J., and Mesa-Bains, A. (eds.). *Diversity in the Classroom: A Casebook for Teachers and Teacher Educators*. Hillsdale, N.J.: Erlbaum, 1993.

3. Berliner, D. "Implications of Studies in Pedagogy for Teacher Education." Paper presented at the Educational Testing Service International Conference on New Directions for Teacher Assessment, New York, October 1988.

4. Ladson-Billings, G. "Returning to the Source: Implications for Educating Teachers of Black Students. In M. Foster (ed.), *Readings in Equal Education*, Vol. 11, 1991, pp. 227–244.

5. Asante, M. K. *The Afrocentric Idea*. Philadelphia: Temple University Press, 1987.

6. Collins, P. *Black Feminist Thought*. New York: Routledge & Paul, 1991.

7. "Afrocentrism: What's It All About?" *Newsweek*, Sept. 23, 1991, pp. 42–50.

8. Ladson-Billings, "Returning to the Source," pp. 235–236.

9. Sirotnik, K. "Studying the Education of Educators: Methodology." *Phi Delta Kappan*, 1991, 70(3), 241.

10. Foster, M. "Constancy, Connectedness, and Constraints in the Lives of African American Women Teachers." *National Association of Women's Studies Journal*, 1991, 3(2), 70–97.

11. McLaren, P. *Life in Schools: An Introduction to Critical Pedagogy in the Foundations of Education*. White Plains, N.Y.: Longman, 1989, 215.

12. Spradley, J. *The Ethnographic Interview*. Troy, Mo.: Holt, Rinehart & Winston, 1979.

13. Berliner, "Implications of Studies," p. 39.

14. Collins, *Black Feminist Thought*, p. 208.

15. Ibid., 208–209.

16. Hooks, B. *Talking Back: Thinking Feminist, Thinking Black*. Boston: South End Press, 1989, 131.

17. Casey, K. *I Answer with My Life: Life Histories of Women Teachers Working for Social Change*. New York: Routledge & Kegan Paul, 1993.

18. Noddings, N. *Caring: A Feminine Approach to Ethics and Moral Education*. Berkeley, Calif.: University of California Press, 1984.

19. Collins, *Black Feminist Thought*, 215.

20. Ibid., 217.

21. Ibid., 218–219.

INDEX

*

A

African American immersion
 schools, 3
Ahlquist, R., 143
Amove, R., 111
Anderson, M., 10
Angelou, M., 139
Appearance and self-esteem of
 teachers, 39–40
Apple, M., 87
Artists, teachers as, 45–48
Assimilationist teaching behaviors,
 24, 25, 38, 60, 89
At-risk children: behaviors toward,
 23 24, 26; as negative term, 9 10
Au, K., 12, 18

B

Baraka, A., 159
Bay Area Writing Project,
 115–116
Behavior patterns of teachers, 23–28
Bell, D., 6, 142
Bennett, W., 153
Bloom, A., 86
Board of Education, Brown vs., 2
Book of the Month Club, 124–125
Boyd, C. D., 117
Brown vs. Board of Education, 2
Bush, G., 120

C

Cartwright, M., 155
Charlie Pippin, 117–119
Chavez, C., 88
Chicago Mastery Learning Reading
 Program, 11
Clifton, L., 88
*Closing of the American Mind,
 The,* 86
Coaches, teachers as, 26–28
Coerr, E., 119
Cohen, E., 8
Collins, M., 27
Community involvement and
 culturally relevant teachers, 41–45
Community of learners, encouraging,
 74–76
Competence of students, 134
Conductors, teachers as, 26–27
Connectedness with each student,
 72–74
Connection to wider communities,
 52–56
Cooperative learning, 65, 76–78
Critical view of knowledge, 99–102
Cuban, L., 9, 10
Cultural appropriateness, 18
Cultural Literacy, 86
Cultural relevance, notion of, 19–20
Cultural synchronization, 19

Culturally relevant school, vision of, 149–156
Culturally relevant teaching: aim of, 25; basics of, 34–58; conceptions of knowledge and, 88–110; general description of, 28–29; literacy and, 111–128; math instruction and, 128–131; opportunities for observation of, 147–148; social relations and, 59–83
Cummins, J., 12
Custodians, teachers as, 24

D
deCastell, S., 112
Delpit, L., 34, 89
Desegregation in schools, impact of, 6–7
Devereaux, J., 41–43, 44, 51, 69–71, 99–100, 113, 121–128, 131, 135, 136, 140
Dorsey-Gaines, C., 19
Dreamkeepers: brief snapshots of new, 157–176; hope and, 176–177; in original study, vii–x
Dreeben, R., 59
Dropout rate, high school, 2
Du Bois, W.E.B., 1, 5
Dupree, P., 38–41, 42, 51, 65, 77, 95, 106, 107, 141
Dysconscious racism, 35

E
Economic and social realities for African Americans, 2
Effective teaching for African Americans, study of, 13–15
Erickson, F., 17
Escalante, J., 27
Excellence, as complex standard, 106–109
Extended self, 75

F
Ferdman, B., 112
Fleming, J., 5
Foster, H., 39

G
Gadsden, V., 112
Gates, H. L., 175
General contractors, teachers as, 23, 24
Giovanni, N., 88
Girl Scouts, 41, 70, 122
Giroux, H., 15, 18
Graff, G., 86
Graff, H., 111
Grant, C., 142
Greenfield, E., 88

H
Hale-Benson, J., 19
Hammer, M. C., 90
Hansberry, L., 159
Harris, E., 49, 50–52, 68–69, 97, 141
Hawkins, C., 139, 140
Hilliard, P., 56–57, 67, 71, 74–75, 88–92, 96
Hirsch, E. D., 86, 87
Historically black colleges and universities (HBCUs), 5–6
Hollins, E. R., 11
Home culture, honoring students', 151–152
Hughes, L., 1, 111

I
Immersion in African American culture for teacher candidates, 146–147
Immersion schools, African American, 3
Instructional scaffolding, 134–135
Irvine, J., 19

J
Jackson, J., 88
Jackson, K., 87
Jackson, P., 59
Joel (from the Bible), 157
Jordan, C., 12, 18

K
King, M. L., 33, 55–56
King Herod, 17
Knowledge: culturally relevant
  conceptions of, 88, 89;
  educational debate over, 85–88; as
  evolutionary process, 88–99
Kozol, J., 139, 140
Kuhn, T., 85

L
Leacock, S., vii
Lewis, A., 43–44, 45, 55–56, 75–76,
  79, 92–94, 95–96, 99, 113–121,
  131, 134, 135, 136, 143
Lipman, P., 142
Literacy: basal-text techniques for,
  121–126; focus on, 111–113;
  revival, 113–121; tenets of literacy
  programs, 126–128
Lomotey, K, 6
Luke, A., 112

M
Mandela, N., 55, 56
Marsalis, W., 171
Marshall, T., 2
Math instruction in culturally
  relevant classroom, 128–131
Matthew (the apostle), 17
McKay, N., 175–176
McLaren, P., 18
Mohatt, G., 17
Moses, B., 175
Motivating teachers,
  142–149

P
Paley, V. G., 34
Parks, R., 65, 66
Passion for knowledge, 102–104
Pedagogy, view of, 15
Permanence of racism, 142
Personal appearance, importance of,
  39–40
Psychological safety, 79

R
Racism: dysconscious, 35;
  permanence of, 142; shielding
  students against, 152–153
Referral agents, 24
Rist, R., 64
Robeson, P., 10
Rossi, M., 53–55, 72–74, 97, 100–101,
  104–105, 128–131, 132, 134, 135,
  136, 141

S
*Sadako and the Thousand Paper
  Cranes*, 119
Sandberg, C., 154
Schlesinger, A., 87
School, vision of a culturally
  relevant, 149–156
School desegregation laws, impact
  of, 6–7
Schools for African Americans:
  new call for, 1, 2; reasons for, 3–5;
  special schooling or separate,
  7–13
Secada, W., 142
Segregation and immersion
  schools, 3
Self-determination, educational,
  150–151
Self-esteem and culturally relevant
  practices, 37–41
Shakespeare, W., 86
Shalala, D., 176

Shulman, L., 29, 103
Simon, R., 15
Sizer, T., 153
Skills, development of necessary, 104–106
Social relations: beyond classroom, 67–71; in community of learners, 74–76; conclusions on, 82–84; connectedness with each student, 72–74; cooperative learning and, 76–78; culturally relevant versus assimilationist, 60–64; teacher-student relationship, 66–67
Spindler, G., 48
Staley, J., 6
Statistics, poor education, 1–2
Steptoe, J., 100
Student teacher's experience (Alex Walsh), lessons from, 131–136
Student teaching assignments, longer, 148–149
Students: believing in, 48–52; building community with, 41–45; as community of learners, 74–76; connecting between wider communities with, 52–56; digging knowledge out of, 56–58; tracking of, 64–66
Students' home culture, honoring, 151–152
Study of effective teaching for African Americans, 13–15
Success of all students, belief in, 48–52
Sunday school, 68–69

T
Taylor, D., 19
Teachers: behavior patterns of, 23–28; motivating, 142–149;

new dreamkeepers, 157–176; perceptions of students and, 20–29; power and responsibility of, 139–142; quality and qualifications, of, 8, 9; reasons for becoming, 102–103; self-esteem of, 37–41; in study, 29–32
Teaching, culturally relevant: aim of, 25; basics of, 34–58; conceptions of knowledge and, 88–110; general description of, 28–29; literacy and, 111–128; math instruction and, 128–131; opportunties for observation of, 147–148; social relations and, 59–83
Teaching for African Americans, study of effective, 13–15
Tracking of students, 64–66
Tutors, teachers as, 23, 24

V
Valentine, P., 45–48, 66, 79–82, 106, 107–108, 141
Values clarification, 79–82
Villegas, A., 18
Vision of a culturally relevant school, 149–156

W
Walker, A., 86
Ward, D. T., 159
West, C., 177
Wilson, A., 159
Winfield, L., 23, 25
Winston, G., 49–50, 76–77, 78, 95, 105–106, 142

DISCUSSION QUESTIONS

1. "No challenge has been more daunting than that of improving the academic achievement of African American students" (p. xv). What has made that task particularly daunting? What efforts have been made to effect such an improvement? Why and how have those efforts succeeded or failed? What efforts for improvement does Ladson-Billings recommend?

2. "If one puts aside the obvious objections to separate schools [for African Americans]," Ladson-Billings writes, "—that they are inequitable, undemocratic, regressive, and illegal—and considers the possible merits, the current calls for separate schools may be understandable" (p. 4). What are the possible merits of separate African American schools and how might they be justified? What are some of the arguments to the contrary?

3. Ladson-Billings notes E. R. Hollins's three broad categories of programs "that have demonstrated a level of effectiveness with African American students . . . those designed to remediate or accelerate without attending to the students' social or cultural needs; those designed to resocialize African American students to mainstream behavior, values, and attitudes at the same time that they teach basic skills; and those designed to facilitate student learning by capitalizing on the students' own social and cultural backgrounds" (p. 11). What might be the values and drawbacks of each type of program? Which types have you experienced or

observed? In your opinion, which type has appeared to be most effective, and why?

4. Ladson-Billings writes that her book "examines effective teaching for African American students and how such teaching has helped students not only achieve academic success but also achieve that success while maintaining a positive identity as African Americans. . . . It is about the kind of teaching that the African American community has identified as having its children's best interests at heart" (pp. 13–14). In what ways does The Dreamkeepers show how this kind of teaching benefits both African American students and communities and why the African American community sees this kind of teaching as most effectively serving its children's interests?

5. How does L. Winfield's cross-classification system of "four possible teacher behavior patterns" (p. 23) help us to understand traditional approaches to teaching African American students and to modify our own assumptions, expectations, and practices? In what ways does the addition of Conductors and Coaches to Winfield's conceptualization expand our perceptions of what is needed and what is possible in regard to students achieving excellence? What expectations, behaviors, and objectives characterize Conductors and Coaches?

6. Ladson-Billings writes: "Although I provide explanations and derivations as a researcher, . . . I anticipate that [teachers and other readers] will suggest other interpretations and explanations because of their own pedagogical situations and contexts" (p. 29). What "other interpretations and explanations" can you suggest as a result of your own experiences and observations? To what extent do they differ from those of the author?

7. What are the basics of culturally relevant teaching as Ladson-Billings identifies them in Chapter Three? What illustrations of these basics does she present throughout The Dreamkeepers and

how appropriate and convincing are those illustrations? What illustrations of the basics can you provide from your own experience and observations?

8. What characteristics of the studied teacher's appearances, behaviors, outlooks, and practices contribute to their success as culturally relevant teachers? How might each characteristic contribute to a teacher's success in guiding African American and other minority students toward excellence?

9. In what ways are a teacher's sense of the students' community, of the students' involvement in that community, and of her or his own interaction with the community important to successful culturally relevant teaching and to the students' advancement? How can teachers build community in their classrooms? How do you see community as important in your own education and in your actual or anticipated practices as a teacher?

10. What are the key differences between culturally relevant and assimilationist approaches to building social relations in the classroom? How might the assimilationist practices be modified or corrected so as to achieve a more culturally relevant context for both teachers and students?

11. What might be the importance of teachers finding ways to facilitate "out-of-school (or at least out-of-the-classroom) interaction" with their students and their students' families and community? (p. 68). How might that kind of interaction be generated? How do you, or how could you, realize such out-of-the-classroom interaction?

12. How does the kind of teaching advocated by the eight profiled teachers "help students see community-building as a life-long practice that extends beyond the classroom"? (p. 78). What examples of such community building can you provide?

13. What are the key differences between culturally relevant and assimilationist conceptions of knowledge? How does the culturally relevant teacher establish and reinforce students' concept and acquisition of knowledge. In what ways is knowledge "an evolutionary process"? (p. 88).

14. In what ways might ensuring students' success mean ensuring the teacher's success? Why might it be important that a teacher's success and sense of satisfaction depend on the success or achievement or her or his students? What are the implications of Margaret Rossi's statement regarding her students: "There is no way for me to have a secure future if they don't have one"? (p. 97).

15. What are some of the ways in which the eight studied teachers involve students' families in class activities? How does such involvement help build classroom and wider communities, foster discovery and construction of knowledge, facilitate the improvement of existing skills and the learning of new ones, reinforce a sense of accomplishment and self-worth among students, and make connections between knowledge and power?

16. Ladson-Billings quotes D. Ferdman as contending that, in a culturally heterogeneous society, literacy "becomes an interactive process that is constantly redefined and renegotiated, as the individual transacts with the socioculturally fluid surroundings" (p. 112). In what ways is literacy "an interactive process" and "a communal activity" (p. 113) in the United States? How do the descriptions of literacy instruction in Ann Lewis's and Julia Devereaux's classrooms illustrate notion of literacy? What illustrations can you provide from your own experience and observations?

17. What are the "overarching tenets" that may be culled from Ann Lewis's and Julia Devereaux's literacy programs? How do those tenets both illustrate and substantiate the benefits of culturally relevant teaching, regardless of specific strategies? In what ways might you incorporate these tenets in your practice?

What additional shared tenets do you see emerging from the two teachers' practices?

18. What does culturally relevant teaching have to do with "questioning (and preparing students to question) the structural inequality, the racism, and the injustice that exist in society"? (p. 140). What instances of inequality, racism, and injustice have you personally experienced or observed, in classrooms and the wider society? What efforts might teachers make to correct those societal and individual failings?

19. In what ways do the eight teachers whom the author studied "practice a subversive pedagogy"? (p. 140). How is the pedagogy of each subversive? In what ways is "working in opposition to the system" the most likely road to success for students and teachers? (p. 140). How does Ladson-Billings suggest we cultivate teaching practices that work in opposition to the system?

20. What recommendations for fostering a rethinking and restructuring of teacher preparation were expressed by the teachers whom Ladson-Billings studied? Which of those recommendations do you find most conducive to the furthering of culturally relevant teaching? What recommendations does Ladson-Billings herself present for making culturally relevant teaching part of education classes and an approach to help all teachers become more effective teachers of African-American students?

21. How might the methodology of Ladson-Billings's study, as explained in Appendix A—and the priorities of that methodology, including the process of teacher selection—have affected the conclusions at which she arrived? How might another methodology have been profitably used? What alternative methodology can you conceive of that would effectively address the issues and concerns that Ladson-Billings set out to address?

This discussion guide was prepared by Hal Hager, of Hal Hager & Associates, Somerville, New Jersey.

Crossing Over to Canaan
The Journey of New Teachers in Diverse Classrooms

By: **GLORIA LADSON-BILLINGS**

ISBN 978-0-7879-5001-9
Hardcover | 192 pp.

"Gloria Ladson-Billings provides a perceptive and interesting account of what is needed to prepare novice teachers to be successful with all students in our multicultural society. This book is must reading for all those entering the profession of teaching today and for those who prepare them for this important work." —**Ken Zeichner**, associate dean and professor of curriculum and instruction, School of Education, University of Wisconsin-Madison

"The multiple voices in Gloria Ladson-Billings' book are compelling, provocative, and insightful-they provide a powerful 'insider' perspective on what it really means to learn to teach all children well." —**Marilyn Cochran-Smith**, professor of education and editor, Journal of Teacher Education, Boston College, School of Education

The author of the best-selling book *The Dreamkeepers* shows how teachers can succeed in diverse classrooms. Educating teachers to work well in multicultural classrooms has become an all-important educational priority in today's schools. In *Crossing Over to Canaan*, Gloria Ladson-Billings details the real-life stories of eight novice teachers participating in an innovative teacher education program called Teach for Diversity. Through their experiences, she illustrates how good teachers can meet the challenges of teaching students from highly diverse backgrounds – and find a way to "cross over to Canaan."

Teaching with Fire

Poetry that Sustains the
Courage to Teach

SAM M. INTRATOR and **MEAGAN SCRIBNER**, editors

ISBN 978-0-7879-6970-7
Hardcover | 256 pp.

"Teaching with Fire *is a glorious collection of the poetry that has restored the faith of teachers in the highest, most transcendent values of their work with children . . . . Those who want us to believe that teaching is a technocratic and robotic skill devoid of art or joy or beauty need to read this powerful collection. So, for that matter, do we all."* —**Jonathan Kozol**, author, *Amazing Grace* and *Savage Inequalities*

Teaching with Fire is a wonderful collection of eighty-eight poems from well-loved poets such as Walt Whitman, Langston Hughes, Billy Collins, Emily Dickinson, and Pablo Neruda. Each of these evocative poems is accompanied by a brief story from a teacher explaining the significance of the poem in his or her life's work. This beautiful book also includes an essay that describes how poetry can be used to grow both personally and professionally.

SAM M. INTRATOR is a professor at Smith College and founder of the Smith College Urban Education Initiative. He is a former high school teacher and administrator and the son of two public school teachers. He is the author/editor of five books, including *Tuned In and Fired Up*, *Leading From Within*, and *Stories of the Courage to Teach*.

MEGAN SCRIBNER is a freelance writer, editor, and program evaluator who has conducted research on what sustains and empowers the lives of teachers. She is the mother of two children and PTA president of their elementary school in Takoma Park, Maryland.

Teaching with Fire was written in partnership with the
Center for Teacher Formation and the Bill & Melinda Gates Foundation.

The First-Year Teacher's Survival Guide

Ready-to-Use Strategies, Tools & Activities for
Meeting the Challenges of Each School Day

2nd Edition

By: **JULIA G. THOMPSON**

ISBN 978-0-7879-9455-6
Paperback | 464 pp.

"Every new teacher of the twenty-first century needs this book! Julia Thompson has skillfully created an invaluable survival guide filled with a wealth of expertise and wisdom to help new teachers through almost every problem they may encounter." —**Sherry Cameron**, sixth-grade resource teacher, Richard B. Wilson K–8 School, Tucson, Arizona

"This book should be mandatory reading for all beginning teachers! Julia Thompson has created an invaluable resource that will empower new teachers with its wealth of practical information, classroom-proven strategies, and wise advice." —**Robin Gardner**, Uniserv director, Virginia Education Association, Richmond, Virginia

The completely revised and updated edition of the best-selling *First-Year Teacher's Survival Kit* offers beginning teachers a wide variety of tested strategies, activities, and tools for creating a positive and dynamic learning environment while meeting the challenges of each school day. The book is filled with valuable tips, suggestions, and ideas for helping teachers with everything from becoming effective team players and connecting with students to handling behavior problems and working within diverse classrooms.

Julia G. Thompson has been a public school teacher for more than twenty-five years. She has taught a wide variety of subjects including English, reading, special education, math, geography, home economics, physical education, and employment skills. She is the best-selling author of Discipline Survival Kit for the Secondary Teacher.

The Trouble With Black Boys

And Other Reflections on Race, Equity, and the Future of Public Education

By: **PEDRO A. NOGUERA**

ISBN 978-0-470-45208-0
Paperback | 352 pp.

"Pedro Noguera has provided here an accessible account of the role race plays in the continuing disenfranchisement of students of color. These essays challenge educators to look at what we can do in schools rather than focus on factors out of our control. Once again Pedro Noguera has cut to the quick with his cogent analyses, research-based findings, and personal stories to change our minds and open our hearts to possibilities." –**Lisa Delpit**, executive director for the Center for Urban Education and Innovation, Florida International University

The Trouble With Black Boys is a brutally honest—yet ultimately hopeful—book in which Pedro Noguera examines the many facets of race in schools and society and reveals what it will take to improve outcomes for all students. One of the nation's most important voices on the subject of equity and social justice in education, Noguera examines the link between racial identity and school-related behavior, the significance of race in the racial achievement gap, and the educational future of Latino immigrants.

He discusses the role of leaders in restoring public faith in education, recommends investing in the social capital of students and their parents, and ultimately proposes how to reclaim the promise of public education. From achievement gaps to immigration, Noguera offers a rich and compelling picture of a complex issue that affects all of us.

Pedro A. Noguera is a professor at the Steinhardt School of Education at New York University, the executive director of the Metropolitan Center for Urban Education, and the co-director of the Institute for the Study of Globalization and Education in Metropolitan Settings (IGEMS).

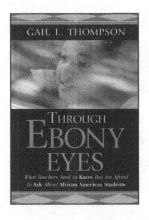

Through Ebony Eyes

What Teachers Need to Know But Are Afraid to Ask
About African American Students

By: **GAIL L. THOMPSON**

ISBN 978-0-7879-8769-5
Paperback | 352 pp.

"Reading this book is like talking with a trusted friend about serious and sensitive issues. Dr. Thompson has provided a real service for teachers and everyone else who cares about the success of African American students." —**Diane F. Halpern**, director, Berger Institute for Work, Family, and Children andprofessor of psychology, Claremont McKenna College

In *Through Ebony Eyes*, Gail L. Thompson takes on the volatile topic of the role of race in education and explores the black-white achievement gap and the cultural divide that exists between some teachers and African American students.

Solidly based on research conducted with 175 educators, *Through Ebony Eyes* provides information and strategies that will help teachers increase their effectiveness with African American students. Written in conversational language, *Through Ebony Eyes* offers a wealth of examples and personal stories that clearly demonstrate the cultural differences that exist in the schools and offers a three-part, long-term professional development plan that will help teachers become more effective.

Gail L. Thompson is associate professor of education at Claremont Graduate University. Her research has focused on the schooling experiences of students of color. She is the author of *African American Teens Discuss Their Schooling Experiences*, *What African American Parents Want Educators to Know*, and *Up Where We Belong*, as well as numerous journal articles.